VEGAN A GO-GO!

A COOKBOOK & SURVIVAL MANUAL FOR VEGANS ON THE ROAD

WITHDRAWN

Sarah Kramer

PULP PRESS

ARSENAL PULP PRESS
Suite 200, 341 Water Street
Vancouver, BC
Canada V6B 1B8
arsenalpulp.com

The publisher gratefully acknowledges the support of the Government of Canada through the Book Publishing Industry Development Program and the Government of British Columbia through the Book Publishing Tax Credit Program for its publishing activities.

The author and publisher assert that the information contained in this book is true and complete to the best of their knowledge. All recommendations are made without guarantee on the part of the author and Arsenal Pulp Press. The author and publisher disclaim any liability in connection with the use of this information. For more information, contact the publisher.

Some of these recipes have been adapted from the books *How It All Vegan!* and *The Garden Of Vegan* by Tanya Barnard and Sarah Kramer, and *La Dolce Vegan!* by Sarah Kramer.

Sarah Kramer's website: GoVegan.net
Book design & art direction by Rudy Penando (*rudeegraphics.co.uk*)
Photography & drawings by Gerry Kramer (*gerrykramer.com*)

Printed and bound in China

Library and Archives Canada Cataloguing in Publication

Kramer, Sarah, 1968-
     Vegan à go-go! : a cookbook & survival manual for vegans on the road / Sarah Kramer.

Includes index.

ISBN 978-1-55152-240-1

  1. Vegan cookery. 2. Vegans--Travel. I. Title.

TX837.K74 2008   641.5'636   C2008-902863-5

This book is dedicated to you.
With love.

thank you

This book may be teeny tiny but the list of people I need to thank is long.... Books of any size are collaborative beasts, so thanks to each and every single one of you who helped with ideas, shared suggestions, tested recipes, and gave me unconditional love and support. You know who you are, and I thank you.

But I do need to call out a few key people. First and foremost my amazing husband Gerry (*gerrykramer.com*), who after a long day of tattooing helped me shoot photos, do drawings, taste recipes, and brainstorm about the book. He is a tireless champion for my success, and I love him more and more every day. To my dog Fergus for helping me live in the now. To my wonderful family and friends for their love and support. Special thanks to Brian and all the crew at Arsenal Pulp Press for their hard work. Thank you to all my *Vagina Monologue* sisters for standing beside me while I found the courage to share. To Heather for putting it all in perspective. A big, giant thanks to Rudee for stepping in and doing an amazing kick ass design for this book. Thanks to Tanya Barnard.

A special thanks to all of my friends in the veggie community who support me both near and far; in particular, Sara and Erica (*mooshoes.com*), Steve (*leftfeet.ca*), Rudee (*secretsocietyofvegans.com*), Bob and Jenna (*veganfreak.net*), Josh, Michelle, and Ruby (*herbivoreclothing.com*), Isa (*theppk.com*), Dan Piraro (*bizarro.com*), and Emiko and Chad (*foodfightgrocery.com*).

Big, wet, sloppy kisses to my pals Jake (*supportjake.org*) and Josh (*joshharper.org*), and lots of love and thanks to all my friends over at the *GoVegan.net* forum. And of course, special thanks to Jane Wiedlin (*janewiedlin.com*) and all The Go-Go's (*gogos.com*) for writing the soundtrack of my life.

A GIANT shout out to *stopstaringclothing.com* for the dresses they provided for the book. To *minkshoes.com* for the beautiful shoes. To *modemerr.com* and *tarantulaclothingcompany.com* for also providing outfits. *Dungareedolly.com* for her wicked purses and her cutie pie face. To *brookadelphia.com* for the bling. To *jeanettezeis.com* for her beautiful vegan ceramics.

And lastly, thanks to you. Yes, YOU! I spend so much time alone in my kitchen daydreaming, writing, testing, re-testing recipes ... so when I get to hear from you about how much you enjoy the books or how they've made your vegan journey a little easier, it's unbelievably fulfilling and brings me great joy. The hugs, stories, and kind words of encouragement you share are not lost on me. Thank you to each and every one of you for your support. You have no idea how happy you make me. You are awesome. This book is a love letter to you. I hope you enjoy it.

contents

Preface

Traveling is exhausting at the best of times, under the best of circumstances. Passports, homeland security, lineups, remembering to bring enough socks, counting out vitamins, yada, yada, yada ... throw veganism into the mix and there's one more thing to worry about. Oy.

In this travel-sized book, you will find some of the most popular recipes from *How It All Vegan!* (*HIAV*), *The Garden of Vegan* (*GOV*), and *La Dolce Vegan!* (*LDV*), as well as some NEW easy and delicious recipes. When you get to your destination you can reach into your suitcase, grab your copy of *Vegan à Go-Go!* (*VAGG*) and wow your friends, family, or travel buddies with your cooking skills, all thanks to this wee book.

How To Use This Book

You can keep this book with your other cookbooks, but I would suggest you stick it in the same safe place you keep your passport and other travel items. That way you'll never forget to shove it in your suitcase when you leave town.

Passport Stamps

These stamps will give you a quick idea of what each recipe is geared for.

New Stamp

These are new—*never before seen*—yumtastic recipes.

Quick & Easy Stamp

Many of the ingredients in these recipes can be found at any grocery store, and these recipes are quick to make.

Travels Well Stamp

These are recipes for surviving that visit to your family who live in Meat-ville and have never seen a soybean, let alone tasted one.

Will Impress Your Friends Stamp

These are recipes that you can make when you want to impress your friends and families with your mad culinary skills.

Needs Special Ingredients Stamp

These recipes require ingredients that you may not be able to find in Meat-ville, but if you come prepared with a few key ingredients in your luggage, you can knock the socks off all the folks who dare to doubt that vegans eat yummy, delicious food.

Last But Not Least

When you see vegan milk or "milk" in quotes, that means use your favorite "milk" alternative (soy, rice, hemp, oat, etc.). *Happy trails!*

Introduction

I love my creature comforts. I love my pillow. I like my bed sheets to be tucked a certain way. I like having a place for everything and everything in its place. I'm a total creature of habit. I like knowing what my day is going to be like before I get out of my pajamas.

And while I love traveling, I dislike the logistics of it all. The packing, the schlepping of heavy bags, late flights, lost luggage, airplane food, flat tires, dirty gas station bathrooms ... and, worst of all, the germs. Other people's germs. *Eeeek!*

While I might come across as a bit of a travel diva, I did not start out this way. As a child, I lived a somewhat nomadic life. In 1966, my parents founded Saskatchewan's first professional theater company, and while Regina was the home base for the theater, the company also toured extensively across the province and performed in communities for school students.

Many of my childhood travel memories are of being on tour with the theater: playing in the back seat, looking wistfully out the window at the prairie landscape, singing *"where, oh where, is the gas station because Sarah has to pee,"* or sleeping curled up on the floor of the car while we drove through the night (this was before seat belt laws).

As a child, I felt that my life was perfectly normal and it wasn't until I got a little older that I realized—not everyone's mother wore a cat costume on stage. I thought that everyone's dad could sword fight and recite *Hamlet*. Not all kids had parents who took them to art galleries or wrote poetry or did yoga with them. None of my schoolmates had parents with friends who could juggle or sculpt cows or write plays. Looking back, it was an unusual life, but one which filled me with so much wonderful creative energy that made me who I am today.

Since my mother was originally from England, we would often travel back and forth to Europe to see her side of the family. I have many memories of riding double-decker buses, exploring castles, and visiting art museum after art museum after art museum. On my dad's side, who lived on the west coast of Canada, we would travel to Lotusland (Vancouver) to visit my Zeyda and then take a ferry to Victoria, on Vancouver Island, to see my Auntie Bonnie and my cousins. Lucky for us, Zeyda also had a condo in Hawaii, so we would frequently escape the dreadful winters of Saskatchewan to explore the warm, breezy tropics of Maui.

As I transitioned from childhood into a sullen teenager, we didn't do a lot of traveling. My mum had passed away a few years earlier, and my dad became more rooted in operating the theater in our hometown. Most of our travels at that time were short family vacations, and throughout almost all of them, I was miserable. Miserable because I was a teenager, yes, but also because I hadn't learned how to take care of myself. I was dependent on others for my happiness and I had yet to realize that despite all the chaos of life, YOU are the captain of your own ship and can point yourself in whatever direction you want.

As I stretched my wings and moved away from home, traveling became more of an adventure. My friends and I would fill up the

car with gas, buy supplies at the corner store, and hit the road with no plans and no idea what was around the bend. It was so exciting.

Sometimes it would just be a quick drive to Regina Beach or, once I moved to Victoria, a full day trip up Vancouver Island to hit some of the thrift stores in Nanaimo (visit page 156 for recipe), or a roadtrip down to Portland, Oregon, with nothing but a credit card, a toothbrush, and a vague idea of which way was south. I went to Vegas more than a few times with nothing but a few $$ in my pocket and the hope that I'd strike it rich—thank goodness the slot machines were always good to me. Then there's the time my roommates and I decided to drive from Victoria to Mexico in a VW bug for Xmas. Exhausted, cranky, and cramped for space, we decided to stop in San Diego and crash at a friend's house for the holidays instead. We did eventually make it to Mexico but only as a day trip to Tijuana, where I was swarmed by a group of small children who picked my pocket ... but that's a story for another day.

Those trips were crazy fun—driving late at night, singing along to Elvis cassettes, feeling drunk from too much sugar, and being so exhausted from the many hours on the road that we got so giddy and crazy. But hindsight is everything. While I was traveling around with my friends, we weren't being very safe. We slept in the car in unfamiliar parking lots, did a lot of couch surfing at random strangers' houses, and, worst of all, I did a little hitchhiking. I was in a lovely little bubble of my own creation and, for a long time, I felt that as long as I had a smile on my face

and a credit card in my pocket nothing could hurt me. Boy, was I wrong.

I've had a long love affair with Elvis and I had always wanted to go to Graceland to visit The King, so one day two girlfriends and I headed to Memphis, Tennessee. We were staying at a friend of a friend's house that was half a block from Sun Records. It was amazing; everywhere we turned we saw something historic. And then, of course, there was the incredible day we spent wandering around Graceland. What a wonderful time we had. Wowzers. So much fun....

After our trip to Memphis, we decided to drive to New Orleans. This was back in the day before the Internet and the punk rock scene was sewn together by word of mouth. You could usually find a place to stay by knowing someone who knew someone who had been where you were going and met someone with a couch to sleep on. So with a hand-drawn map from a friend and some rough directions to a punk house to crash at, we hit the road.

New Orleans was dark by the time we arrived. We drove around and around trying to find the punk house—only to find ourselves completely lost. We stopped at a gas station, got some directions, and *voilà!* We found the house and knocked on the door, but there was no answer. We stood in the street trying to figure out what to do or where to go next. I looked around at all the cute little houses with their cute little porches. The neighborhood looked a little rough around the edges but not any rougher than the punk house where I was living in Victoria. We knocked on the door one last time but still no answer. *Now what?*

A man drove by us on a bicycle, then he did a U-turn, hopped off his bike, and asked us if we needed directions. My gut instinct was to run. I had this funny, nagging feeling ... but instead I smiled and showed him our crude directions. He asked us if we were looking for some "punky girls" who lived in this house; we were so thrilled he knew who we were talking about.

The next thing I knew I had a gun in my face, a hand on my throat, and we were in serious trouble. The man wanted our wallets. *Fine, take them.* Then he wanted to go through our suitcases. *Fine, go ahead.* Look in the trunk. *Fine*. Then he wanted to go through our pockets. That's when things got crazy. He got rough. He was mean. He threatened us. Hurt us.

When he was done assaulting us, he took our car keys, had us take off our shoes, and made us lie on the ground. I knew we were dead. I was ready for it. I reached for my friend's hand, squeezed it with all my might, and closed my eyes. I didn't want to die, but I knew it was coming. What came instead was a blow to the head. He hit us with the butt of his gun, got into our car, and drove away. I looked up and watched in disbelief as the taillights of our car rounded the corner and disappeared. Was I alive? Were we shot? Was everyone OK? I was in a daze as I watched my friends scramble to put their shoes on. My body was frozen and I couldn't think. I was in shock. Completely shut down. I could not comprehend what had happened and couldn't move until my girlfriends grabbed my hands and dragged me up the street, yelling at me to run. Somehow we managed to make it to the main road to find help. We flagged down a security car whose driver called the police who then called an ambulance.

We went to the hospital, had our wounds tended, filled out a police report, and canceled our credit cards. The robber had taken everything we owned and now we were stuck in the South with no money, no clothing, no passports, nothing. Then I called my parents. Heartbroken and emotionally wrecked, I was immediately lifted up by the support of my stepmum. She quickly wired us some money so we could buy necessities like socks, toothbrushes, underwear, et cetera. She was amazing.... She is amazing.

Now, it was time to call home to Gerry. I left this call for last because this was the one I was dreading the most; I knew I was going to break down when I heard Gerry's voice, and I wasn't ready yet. I had to keep it together. I had to get us home. Nobody answered at the house. *Ha.* I left a message on the machine for our roommates, but because I didn't want to freak them out, I tried to make it sound casual: "Hey. We were robbed. I'm at the hospital and we're all OK. I'll call back later." Because cell phones were not yet commonplace, I asked them to tell Gerry about what happened and let him know that I was OK and that I would call back as soon as I could.

As I left the message, I absentmindedly watched a janitor mop and clean the hallway. I hung up the phone and gave him a smile as I started to head back to the ER to check on my friends. He quickly ran over and passed me a five-dollar bill and said he hoped it would help. I fell apart. His kindness was overwhelming.

I went back to the nurses' station and explained that we were stranded with *nothing* and were desperate. They immediately got on the phone and helped get us a free hotel room. They also handed me a pile of scrubs for us to wear. We seemed to be surrounded by guardian angels, and I took great comfort in their kindness.

The next morning, the police called us at the hotel and told us they had found our car. They picked us up (I got to sit in the back like a criminal, *eeek*) and drove us to the vacant lot. The car was wrecked. It had been unsuccessfully set on fire so it stunk like burnt chemicals and booze. Luckily, the engine still worked, so we got in the car and drove to the police station where they helped us get the necessary paperwork to get back over the border to Canada. Then we hit the road and hauled our broke-down asses home at lightning speed.

It wasn't until the ferry pulled into the harbor in Victoria that I realized how damaged I was. Now safely at home, my body finally started to let me process what had happened and it wasn't pretty. I was a mess. I headed straight for therapy and started working on my stuff, and I have to say that it's the best thing I ever did. Not only did it help me work through the robbery but it also allowed me to process and understand that it wasn't my fault. We may have been traveling in an unsafe way but we didn't deserve what happened.

This might sound bizarre, but the robbery kick-started my life. Before the robbery, I was just wandering aimlessly, watching life pass me by. After the robbery, I had a thirst for life that I couldn't quench. I wanted to do something positive, fun, and creative with my life, and when my former coauthor, Tanya, came to me with the idea to do a cookbook, I knew immediately we were on to something special.

As it came time to start promoting the first book, **How It All Vegan!**, I had a difficult time getting back out on the road. I was gun-shy, literally. Out of fear, I had spent many years not doing any traveling, and the thought of putting myself back out on the road was scary, to say the least. But I had a book to promote, so I jumped back in with both feet and what a joy it was. Having the chance to meet and greet readers at book signings and cooking demos across North America helped me feel more comfortable about being back on the road again. Slowly but surely I started to feel more secure and confident about traveling. Now this travel diva needs to stay safe, and if that means hopping from hotel to hotel rather then from couch to couch, so be it.

My reason for sharing my robbery story is two-fold. One, is that I want you to know that you can survive anything as long as you seek out the proper support. Help is everywhere (ask your doctor or a trusted friend for a referral, or look in your local Yellow Pages), and finding a safe, positive place to share is so important to promote healing so you can move forward in your life. Two, I want to remind you to *always listen to your instincts*, especially when you're away from home and out of your comfort zone. It's vital as travelers to stay safe, but it's especially important for women travelers to have a good and solid safety plan.

Most importantly, what I've learned is that life is for living, so while my experience changed me in ways that I can't adequately put into words, I didn't let it define or confine me. I love my life and my life loves me back. I live without fear or shame, and while I now tread a little more cautiously when I'm away from home, I am still ready and willing to enjoy the bumps along the road.

So my friends, keep your tank full and the rubber side down. Let's hit the road!

XO XO

Sarah

"No matter what, I want to continue living
with the awareness that I will die.
Without that, I am not alive.
That is what makes the life I have now possible."

BANANA YOSHIMOTO (from Kitchen)

Travel Tips

The way I travel now is different since my experience in New Orleans, and this book may be filled with travel tips that seem obvious to seasoned travelers, but there may be some information in here that will make your travels easier.

I also haven't had an opportunity to travel overseas since the 1980s, when my dad was paying for the ticket. (*Laugh.*) So most of my adult travel experience has been in North America. But traveling is traveling, and schlepping your bags for a month-long trek in Katmandu or for an overnighter in Seattle can take just as much pre-planning and effort.

Thanks to the Internet, the world is at our fingertips, and there are some great resources for vegans. But no matter how well a trip is planned, traveling is completely unpredictable. So rather than freak out when tofu starts to hit the fan, I've devised a few ways to get through all the rigors of traveling and keep my tummy full so I'm less likely to get cranky when plans inevitably fall apart.

Plan Ahead Before You Leave

Before I leave town, I always hit The Google for information about the place(s) I'm going to visit. I check out what kinds of food are available, how safe the area is, and what kind of historical places there are to visit. I love to plan, plan, and plan some more—but once I actually arrive at my destination, I like to let go and see where the town takes me. By doing so, sometimes I end up finding a great hole-in-the-wall café that makes the best veggie burgers that wasn't on my to-do list.

Check out websites like *happycow.net* or *vegdining.com* before you leave on your trip so you'll know how veggie-friendly your destination will be; that way, you'll know if you need to bring an extra suitcase full of supplies. I also always have an energy bar (see pg 157-158) or a small bag of nuts and seeds in my bag in case I can't find food right away. Nobody likes a cranky, hungry Sarah. She's mean.

I print out maps and directions to the places where I want to eat before I leave on my trip so I have a good understanding of where they are geographically in relation to where I'm staying. For your travels, also be on the lookout for different veggie directories for the city you're visiting. For example, if you go to New York, there's a fantastic book called *The Vegan Guide to New York City* by Rynn Berry. You can purchase it online or visit *mooshoes.com* to pick up a copy. The Toronto Vegetarian Association (*veg.ca*) has a pamphlet that you can download that lists all the local veggie-friendly places to visit in Toronto. Even my childhood hometown of Regina has a veggie community (*reginavegetariansociety.org*). Jump online and see what's out there before you leave—you might be pleasantly surprised.

Vegan Passport

Eating out is a challenge at the best of times, but when you're far away from home or in a country where you don't speak the language, ordering food can be extra daunting. There is a fabulous book published by the Vegan Society called the *Vegan Passport*: it's small enough to slip into your pocket when you go out to eat, yet it includes 93% of the languages of the world's population. Each page is in a different language, and not only does it say "I am a vegan" but it also explains what you do and do not eat. It's a MUST HAVE for any traveler. It's available from the *vegansociety. com* store as well as *foodfightgrocery.com*.

Here's five different ways to say "I am a vegan," courtesy of *Vegan Passport*:

1. French: *Je suis vègan (vegetalien).*
2. German: *Ich ernähre mich vegan.*
3. Italian: *Io sono vegano.*
4. Spanish: *Soy vegano/vegana.*
5. Canadian: *I'm vegan, eh.*

I'm Allergic

Not everyone knows what the word vegan means, even if you're in an English-speaking country. If you don't want to get into a complicated conversation about veganism with your server, it's often easier to just say, "I don't eat meat, chicken, and fish, and I'm allergic to all dairy products." List the dairy you don't eat (cheese, milk, butter, etc.) because sometimes they don't think cheese or butter counts as dairy. (*Huh?*)

Don't Freak Out

If you haven't had a chance to check out your destination restaurant beforehand, you may be surprised what you can find there. If it seems that the menu is full of only meat and fish, don't freak out. A lot of dishes (like pasta) can be "veganized" with a quick omission of ingredients. Politely discuss your dietary needs with your server. If there is nothing on the menu that is vegan or can be veganized, you can ask your server if the chef can make you something special. If the kitchen isn't slammed with orders, ask to have a quick conversation with the chef to ensure that they know what you can't or won't eat. If language is a problem, your handy-dandy *Vegan Passport* can be a great help. And don't forget to generously tip both the server and the chef for taking good care of you.

Repeat Business

Restaurants count on word of mouth and your repeat business, so if you end up having a fabulous experience, tell all your friends, or hop onto *happycow.net* or *vegdining.com* and write a review.

Get Crafty

I can't tell you how many times I've been stranded at a hotel surrounded by no amenities except for a drugstore, or how many times I've filled my boots with those complimentary peanut butter packages they leave on the tables at diners, *wink, wink*. Get crafty, my friends. Get crafty!!

Sometimes, you have to depend on the kindness of strangers. I was once stranded at a hotel café in Regina, Saskatchewan and there was NOTHING on the menu for me to eat except toast. I started talking to the café manager about my situation and we ended up having a great conversation about life and veganism. During the conversation, I told him I was about to fly back home but had no food for the plane, and he asked what he could make me. He said they didn't have a lot of vegetables (what kind of restaurant has no vegetables?), but he ran out to a store and bought me an avocado (what a guy!) and managed to put together a sandwich for my flight home. I was deeply touched and will be forever grateful for his kindness. Thanks, Brisdan. Go Riders!

Stick To Ethnic

Ethnic foods can be your saving grace when you're traveling. Indian, Thai, Middle Eastern, and Mexican cuisines all use beans and veggies, and with a quick conversation with your server, you may be surprised to see there is more on the menu to eat than you first thought. Just make sure lard, chicken stock, or ghee isn't used. Many Asian restaurants serve mock meat dishes made from soy or wheat gluten. This is also where the *Vegan Passport* can come in handy if language is an issue.

Oh Boy! Soy!

You'd be surprised how many fast food joints are now serving veggie burgers or veggie dogs. Just ask your server to check the ingredients or, better yet, ask them if you can check the ingredients. Every restaurant is legally bound to have an ingredients book on hand, so don't take no for an answer. It's your right as a customer to look at it because egg, whey powder, etc. are sometimes hidden ingredients in "veggie" products.

BYOF

Bring your own food. I bring all sorts of treats on my trips, but I always make sure that they're up for the trip; crackers, nuts, seeds, and fruit like apples or oranges, and a jar of nut butter (sealed in a Ziploc bag) can sustain a bit of jostling. You can even carry a single-serving soy or rice milk Tetra Pak if you like. Don't forget that you can't bring your produce into some countries, so make sure you eat it before you hit the customs lineup.

I'm also a big fan of Vega Bars (*myvega.com*). I put a box in my suitcase when I travel so I'll always have one to put in my purse to tide me over if I can't find food. The thing I like best about these bars is that they were designed by a vegan, they're easily digestible (some bars leave me so bloated as heck), and they really hit the spot when you're in a pinch.

Airline Tips

On shorter trips, most airlines no longer provide meals but they do have snacks for sale. Most of the time, the snacks are not vegan or even healthy, so I always bring my own snack food (just in case), but I do still check what the airline has to offer. I once had a flight to Toronto where the snack-pack had soygurt, fresh fruit, and sunflower butter with crackers. What an unexpected treat!

My favorite snacky foods for flights are: apples, sugar peas, chickpeas, baby carrots, raisins, nuts, and seeds.

If you're on a longer flight, a meal may be provided, and in that case you should pre-order your vegan meal at least forty-eight hours before flying. Don't trust your online choice; give the airline a call and double check with a human that you're ordering a strict vegan meal. Even when a meal is provided, I always bring a sandwich (see pg 87), just in case.

Ice Ice Baby
A small (or large) icebox can be a blessing on long road trips.

Cruise Tips
If you're headed for a cruise ship, my friends The Wimmers (*planetwimmer.com*) shared a few tricks that can make your floating adventure a little easier:

✳ Speak to the cruise agent or travel agent before you plan your trip to make sure the cruise can accommodate you.

✳ Speak to the chef as soon as you get on board to discuss your dietary needs (often, they have veggie burgers and other veggie items in the pantry that they don't offer to the general guests unless asked).

✳ If you're tired of the buffet and want a sit-down meal, give the chef twenty-four hours' notice so they can prepare a special menu.

✳ Ethnic-themed restaurants on the ship have more choices for vegans, but always ask about hidden ingredients.

✳ Bring Tupperware so you can take the leftovers with you. You're paying for it, so you might as well stock up.

Make Your Own Food

Whenever possible, try to stay with friends or rent an apartment or hotel with a kitchenette. That way if you can't find any suitable restaurants, you can hit the local markets, make your own food, and save $$.

Check Out The Scene

I always try to hit the local health food stores in the places I visit. It's a great place to meet like-minded people, get the scoop on the local scene, and find out about places to eat or hang out.

Don't Panic

If you can't find a restaurant and there isn't a health food store in sight, don't panic (see also Don't Freak Out, pg 23). If you're in North America, you can almost always find a jar of peanut butter, a banana, and a loaf of bread. Almost any grocery store, even a corner store will have something you can eat. Let me tell you about the time I ate a can of chickpeas for dinner ... I also had to buy a can opener.

Note: My pal Sinead does a lot of traveling for work and tells me that peanut butter isn't widely available in Europe except in some Turkish or sometimes Indian grocery stores, so keep that in mind when you're traveling in that direction. These stores are also great places to find vegan-friendly foods, and they carry lots of snackable legumes, like roasted chickpeas, lentils, and the like. Thanks for the hot tip, Sinead!!

Be Prepared

I always have a plastic fork, spoon, and knife in my travel bag for "just in case." There's nothing worse than making a PB & banana sandwich with your fingers.

Other Travel Issues

Always check with the airline before you bring questionable items on board. These days even tweezers can be considered a weapon, so I always double check before I head out because the security rules change on a daily basis. A lot of airlines/airports have information online about what is/isn't acceptable.

Staying Healthy While Traveling

❋ **Moist towelettes:** In case you can't get to a washbasin there are these amazing towel tablets that I love for when I travel. Made by Body Bumps (*bodybumps.com*), they come in a roll of ten and are the size of a mint candy (but don't eat them!). To use, place a tablet in the cap of a water bottle and pour a half ounce of water over it. The towel expands in front of your eyes and *voilà!* You now have a moist towel to wash yourself with. Alternatively you can also carry individually packaged moist towelettes or a travel-sized package of baby wipes, or you could GO GREEN like my stepmum and carry a wet facecloth in a Ziploc baggie. She recently told me that in Europe a good facecloth is hard to come by. Good to know....

❋ **Neti pot:** Usually ceramic, but you can get light plastic travel ones at any health food store or online. After spending time in an airplane, bus, or in any sort of group travel situation, I flush out my nose with a saline solution using my neti pot. It clears my nasal passages and helps promote a healthy sinus cavity. It's also fantastic if you suffer from seasonal allergies or sinus colds. Just Google "neti pot" and then buy one. It will change your life, I swear.

✱Motion sickness wristband: Look like an indie-rocker and help combat motion sickness all at the same time!

✱Tissues: I never touch the inside of my nose unless I'm using a tissue. Your nasal passages are like the doorway to your health—keeping them free of germs is key. Also, I never touch my face with my hands. I am convinced this keeps me from getting sick (along with washing my hands with soap and water). And whenever possible, I don't touch door knobs, chair arms, escalator railings, or even elevator knobs with my hands. (*Hmmmm*, maybe I should start traveling with rubber gloves.)

✱Multi-vitamins: I also take extra vitamin C to help boost my immune system when I'm traveling. I especially like the single-serving packages of vitamin C powder to add to a bottle of water.

Just In Case You Get Sick

Being sick sucks and being sick away from home without any sort of recourse is even worse. I like to have all these items in my bag for "just in case," and they all come in travel sizes: single-serving packages of Emergen-C; echinacea tea bags; Kleenex; something for upset tummies/diarrhea, headaches, and pain; and heat-therapy back patches (also good for cramps). Also, the neti pot has completely changed my life when I get sick (see above).

Things In Sarah's Travel Bag

✱Rescue Remedy (*rescueremedy.com*): I have a little bottle that I spritz in my mouth before takeoff and landing or during any times of stress. Keeps me mellow. I also use it before I go to bed to help relax my restless legs. It is also available in a lozenge, in case you're worried about taking liquid on the plane.

❋**Cocoa butter stick**: Since liquids on planes seem to be a problem these days, I carry a cocoa butter stick and use it for my lips, my hands, my face, and any other parts of my body that need a little moisturizing.

❋**Toiletries**: I carry all my "if I was lost on a desert island" toiletry items in my carry-on bag because if your luggage is lost, at least you'll smell good and look cute in yesterday's clothes.

❋**Extra underwear**: One pair of underwear does not take up a lot of room, and if something happens en route (see above) you'll be thanking the pantie gods that you brought them.

❋**A couple of pads**: Nothing is worse than waking up in the middle of the night to discover your period has arrived ahead of schedule (see above).

❋**Travel laundry soap**: You can buy individual packages of laundry soap for "just in case" (see above).

❋**Something for pain**: My pal Rudee once had to endure a ten-hour plane ride and a major toothache. Not fun.

❋**Ear plugs. Eye mask. Neck pillow.** (A godsend while traveling.)

❋**Travel slippers** (a.k.a. "pee slippers"): hotel room carpets and floors of airplanes are dirty with a capital D! Slippers protect your feet from wayward *stranger pee* and will keep your feet cozy at the same time. Return them to a Ziploc baggie so they don't touch anything else in your bag. *Bleech.*

❋**Chargers**: Don't forget your phone, MP3 player, camera, and/or computer chargers and batteries.

Avoid Jet Lag

It's impossible to completely avoid jet lag when you're changing time zones, but here are some do's to make the transition a little easier.

Do's

❋ Get plenty of sleep and try to be stress-free before you travel—give yourself plenty of time to pack and get your passport, maps, and itinerary all squared away in advance so you're not in a stressful rush before you leave.

❋ Set your watch to your destination's time and try eating and sleeping at your destination's scheduled times a day or two before your departure.

❋ Water. Water. Water. Drink at least eight ounces of water every hour. No soda, alcohol, or caffeine, just water.

❋ Eat fresh. Only eat foods that promote health.

❋ Sleep as much as you can.

❋ Exercise. Get up and walk around when you can. Stretch. Do butt clenches in your seat. Do anything to get your blood pumping.

❋ Be comfortable. Wear loose, comfortable clothing so you can chill.

❋ If it's daytime when you arrive at your destination, take a walk—get some sunlight on your body so you can start to adjust to the time difference.

Stay Safe

There are a few things you can do to stay safe when you're traveling. Most of them involve using common sense and listening to your gut. Don't worry about being rude or difficult with people if your safety is at stake. For example, if the hotel room you've reserved feels unsafe because it's on the ground floor, ask for a different room. If the man beside you on the airplane is being inappropriate, ask a flight attendant to change your seat. That funny feeling you may be ignoring is your radar and it's going off for a reason. Always listen to your gut.

Also:

- Take a self-defense course.
- Call home as soon as you arrive at your destination so everyone knows you're groovy.
- Never take anything across the border for anyone (*duh*).
- Don't keep all your traveler's checks in one place.
- If staying in a hotel ask for a room on a higher floor.
- Check that all the doors and windows lock properly. Contact the front desk if they don't and change rooms if need be.
- Place the Do Not Disturb sign on the door.
- Don't open the door to any strangers, even if it's a hotel employee. Call the front desk to see if it's a scheduled visit.
- Lock away any valuables if you need to leave them in your room.
- Ask hotel/hostel staff about areas of town to avoid.
- Don't get wasted. Keep your wits about you.
- Don't carry all your cash with you. Credit cards and traveler's checks are replaceable and traceable if they are stolen.
- Keep your valuables out of sight whenever possible.

Travel Insurance

Just spend the $$ and get it. You never know what's going to happen and it's worth every penny if something does. Make sure the insurance you get has twenty-four hour, seven-days-a-week service and multi-language assistance.

Tell Someone Where You're Going
Keep your friends and family in the know. Pass on your itinerary and any necessary contact info and occasionally check in with them if you have a change of plans, so if something happens they'll be able to track you down.

Keep A Copy
Photocopy all your identification. Give one copy to a trusted family member or friend and keep another copy in your suitcase in case you lose your wallet. Also keep a copy of all your credit cards, as well as the toll-free or collect telephone numbers to call in case you lose them.

Clean Out Your Wallet
And while you're photocopying your ID, take a few minutes to clean out your wallet. Remove any items that are not imperative for your trip and put them in a safe place for when you get home. The less stuff you have, the less you have to replace if your wallet goes missing.

Check The Weather Before You Leave
Did I ever tell you about the time I went to NYC in October anticipating freezing my ass off and instead the weather was so hot that the winter jacket I brought made me sweat so much I felt faint? 'Nuff said.

Traveler's Checks
Replaceable and traceable if stolen. Whoever invented these deserves a kiss.

Stay Entertained

Besides music, I like to fill up my iPod with podcasts to keep me entertained. Check out the *veganfreakradio.com* archives. If you live in Canada (or are a fan of Canadian pop culture), don't forget to check out the CBC's website. They have great shows online at *cbc.ca/podcasting* (*Q, Go!, The Hour,* and *DNTO* are my favs). Lastly, don't forget a good trashy magazine to help pass the time, but avoid reading porn in public.

Stay Comfortable

It's important to stay comfortable, especially if you're stuck sitting in one seat for many hours. But for the love of tofu, people, don't wear your pajamas on the plane. Try to stay a little fashionable while still being comfortable.

Dummy Check

I do a dummy check every time I leave my destination. I pack up everything, put it by the door and then go through the hotel room or friend's house and check every nook and cranny for anything I've forgotten. Check under the bed, in all the drawers, in outlets for phone chargers, or in the bathroom for your razor. Doing a dummy check has saved me too many times to count.

Graze All Day

I try to graze all day so I don't get super hungry and NEED FOOD NOW because if you can't find food right away that's when Sarah starts getting cranky. It's better to top her up throughout the day and then everyone's happy.

Keep An Eye Out For Ghost Bag

Ghost bag follows me everywhere I go. He's usually stuck in a tree or floating around on the ground and sometimes he's a different color but most of the time he's white. It's so dang exciting when I spot him.

Zen Moments

Traveling is stressful, so when you find yourself freaking out, take a Zen moment to yourself. Take a deep, cleansing breath and find something to enjoy. Whether it's the sound of a bird, an interesting piece of architecture, or a giant mole on the face of the woman who is giving you a hard time. Just stop and Zen-out for a moment—you're on a journey and sometimes it's the bumps in the road that make for the best memories. You might as well enjoy the ride!

Sarah's Top Five Restaurants

1. HanGawi: New York City (*hangawirestaurant.com*)
2. Red Bamboo: New York City (*redbamboo-nyc.com*)
3. Cha-Ya: Berkeley (1686 Shattuck Ave., 510-981-1213)
4. Fresh: Toronto (*juiceforlife.com*)
5. LIVE Organic Food Bar: Toronto (*livefoodbar.com*)

Sarah's Top Five Shops

1. MooShoes: New York City (*mooshoes.com*)
2. Left Feet: Toronto (*leftfeet.ca*)
3. Herbivore: Portland, Oregon (*herbivoreclothing.com*)
4. Food Fight! Grocery: Portland, Oregon (*foodfightgrocery.com*)
5. Tattoo Zoo: Victoria, British Columbia (*tattoozoo.net*)

Sarah's Top Five Books (to keep you entertained while traveling)

1. *Herbivore Magazine*, travel issue #14
2. *Vegan Freak* by Bob and Jenna Torres
3. Anything by Douglas Coupland
4. Anything by Banana Yoshimoto
5. Anything by Scarlett Thomas

Recipes

Now before you dive into the recipes, let's take a moment to remember that when you're away from home, try your best to not get frustrated by the food limitations of where you're visiting; instead, look at it as a challenge and a chance to stretch your culinary imagination.

If you can't find tofu, perhaps adding a can of beans to your meal would work just as well. Or maybe making seitan from scratch (pg 187) is something you and your family could do together, and perhaps it will promote a positive conversation about your lifestyle and they can get to know you on a whole different level.

While food is the fuel that keeps our bodies alive and running—preparing and sitting down to a meal with people we love, or even people we just met, is a golden opportunity for us to connect and to pass ideas back and forth while we pass the peas. Enjoy!

Breakfast

Mango Parsley & Freshness Juices

Victoria Boutenko, author of *Green for Life* (*rawfamily.com*), has kindly given me permission to re-publish two of my favorite juice recipes from her book. While Victoria uses a powerful Vita-Mix blender, these two recipes work well if you only have a regular blender or food processor.

Mango Parsley

This recipe is one of my favs from Green for Life. *Gerry and I have it every morning with our breakfast.*

- 2 fresh mangos or 2 cups frozen mango, chopped
- 1 bunch parsley
- 2 cups water

Blend all ingredients together until smooth. Drink immediately. Makes 2 large or 4 small servings.

Freshness

You will love this juice for breakfast, but also try it for lunch or dinner. It's a great way to get your greens without the hassle of chewing. I've requested this recipe at restaurants when they don't have much on their menu for me to eat.

- 8 leaves Romaine lettuce
- ½ medium honeydew
- 2 cups water

Blend all ingredients together until smooth. Drink immediately. Makes 2 large or 4 small servings.

Vegan Freak Curry Potatoes

I discussed this recipe in episode #67 of *Vegan Freak Radio* (*veganfreakradio.com*) and have had requests for it ever since. Ask and ye shall receive. I live to make you happy. If you're somewhere where you can't find tofu, try throwing in half a small can of beans instead (your choice). It's all about adapting to your environment, people.

- 16–20 new potatoes, quartered
- 1 tbsp oil
- 1 tbsp mustard seeds
- 2 tsp curry powder
- 1 cup firm tofu, cubed
- 1–2 tbsp Braggs (or tamari or vegetable stock)
- 3 kale leaves, chopped
- ⅓ cup frozen peas
- salt (to taste)
- black pepper (to taste)
- oil (e.g., flax or hemp)

In a large frying pan on medium heat, sauté the potatoes in the 1 tbsp oil along with the mustard seeds, curry, tofu, and Braggs. Cover with lid and sauté until potatoes are cooked, tossing often to avoid sticking. Toss in the kale and peas. Turn off heat, cover with lid, and let sit 5 minutes before serving. Add salt, pepper, and oil to taste. Makes 2 servings.

Multigrain Porridge

Sticks to your ribs and keeps you going until lunch. I like to serve it with fresh fruit, a splash of vegan milk, maple syrup, or a pinch of stevia.

- 3½ cups water
- ½ cup quinoa
- ½ cup buckwheat groats
- ½ cup cream of rice or cream of wheat
- ½ tsp salt

In a medium saucepan on high heat, bring the water to a boil. Reduce heat to simmer and stir in the quinoa, groats, cream of rice, and salt. Cover and simmer for 15 minutes or until quinoa is cooked. Makes 2 large servings.

SSOV Apple Breakfast for Agents on the Run

If you're a member of the SSOV (*secretsocietyofvegans.co.uk*), then you already know that it doesn't exist. You don't know us but we know you. We exist in secret and work anonymously. This recipe comes from an SSOV Level 3 member. I am a Level 6. *Shhh.* It's a secret.

- 1 Granny Smith apple
- peanut butter
- raisins

Slice apple into thick slices. Spread each apple slice with peanut butter and garnish with raisins. Wait for further instructions from The Top Level Vegan Strategist. Makes 1 serving.

Brainless Banana Pancakes

Brainless Banana Pancakes from *HIAV* is a winner! This had the most votes for fan favorite recipe.

- 1 cup flour
- 2 tsp baking powder
- 1 banana
- 1¼ cups vegan milk
- 1 tbsp sugar
- sliced fresh fruit (for garnish)
- maple syrup (for garnish)

In a large bowl, sift the flour and baking powder together. In a small bowl, mash the banana with a fork and add ¼ cup of the "milk," mixing together until there are no lumps. Add the mashed banana, sugar, and remaining "milk" to the dry mix and stir together until just mixed. Portion out about ¾–1 cup batter onto a hot non-stick frying pan or a lightly oiled frying pan and cover with a lid. Let sit on medium heat until the center starts to bubble and becomes sturdy. Flip pancake over and cook other side until golden brown. Repeat process until all the batter is gone. Garnish with fresh fruit and maple syrup. Makes 2 or more servings.

Freedom French Toast

The best tip for this recipe is to use stale bread. Alternatively, leave some bread out overnight or lightly toast it before cooking. This is one of my all time favorite recipes to make for friends. Their eyes become as big as saucers with the first bite. I love it!!

- ¾ cup soft or silken tofu
- 2 tbsp maple syrup
- ¾ tsp cinnamon
- ½ tsp vanilla extract
- ¼ tsp salt
- ¼ cup apple juice or water
- 1 tbsp oil
- 4–6 large slices bread, stale

With a blender or food processor, blend the tofu, syrup, cinnamon, vanilla, salt, apple juice, and oil until smooth. In a large shallow bowl, pour batter; dip bread slices into batter and coat both sides. Fry in a hot non-stick pan or a lightly oiled hot frying pan and cover. Let sit on medium heat until underside is golden brown. Flip toast over and cook other side until golden brown. Repeat process until bread is gone. Makes 2 large or 4 small servings.

Apple Pie Pancakes

Make this recipe for your gramma next time you visit, she'll have all these ingredients and besides, doesn't she deserve some pancake love?

- ¾ cup flour
- ¼ cup rolled oat flakes
- ½ tsp cinnamon
- 2 tsp baking powder
- ¼ tsp salt
- 1 cup vegan milk
- ¼ cup raisins
- ½ large apple, diced

In a medium bowl, stir together the flour, oat flakes, cinnamon, baking powder, and salt. Add the "milk," raisins, and apples and stir together gently until just mixed. Portion batter onto a hot non-stick pan or a lightly oiled hot frying pan on medium heat and cover with lid. Let sit until the center starts to bubble and becomes sturdy. Flip pancake over and cook other side until golden brown. Repeat process until batter is used. Makes 2 large or 4 small pancakes.

Orange Poppy Seed Pancakes

This recipe rocks my frigging world! —Clinton, Calgary, Alberta

- 1 cup flour
- ½ tsp baking powder
- ½ tsp baking soda
- ¼ tsp salt
- ½ cup rolled oat flakes
- 1 tsp orange zest, grated
- ½ cup sunflower seeds
- ¼ cup poppy seeds
- 1 cup vegan milk
- ⅓ cup orange juice

In a medium bowl, stir together the flour, baking powder, baking soda, salt, oat flakes, orange zest, sunflower seeds, and poppy seeds. Add the "milk" and juice and stir until just mixed. Portion out about ¾–1 cup batter onto a hot non-stick pan or lightly oiled hot frying pan on medium heat and cover with lid. Let sit until the center starts to bubble and becomes sturdy. Flip pancake over and cook other side until golden brown. Repeat process until batter is used. Makes 2 or more servings.

Vegetable Tofu Scrambler

What a great idea ... every time I leave home, I'm scribbling down a recipe or two to take along with me as I'm running out the door. It will be great to have a take-a-long recipe book. I can't live without Veggie Tofu Scrambler!
—Karen, Northwood, New Hampshire

- 1 small onion, chopped
- 4–5 mushrooms, sliced
- 1 tbsp oil
- 1 lb (455 g) firm tofu, crumbled

- 1–2 tsp curry powder
- black pepper (to taste)
- salsa (to taste)
- 2 green onion stalks, chopped

In a large saucepan on medium-high heat, add the onions and mushrooms to the oil and sauté until onions are translucent. Add tofu, curry, and pepper. Sauté 10–12 minutes until moisture has evaporated. Add salsa and green onions and scramble on high heat for 2–4 minutes. Note: You could also add any other veggies you have kicking around. Makes 2 or more servings.

Breakfast Couscous

Couscous can be found in most grocery stores. It's a great quick alternative grain to rice when you're super strapped for time.

- ¾ cup vegan milk or water
- ¼ cup juice (e.g., apple, cranberry, or orange)
- ½ cup couscous
- 1 banana, sliced
- ¼ tsp cinnamon

In a small pot on high heat, bring the "milk" and juice to a boil. Reduce heat and stir in couscous, banana, and cinnamon. Cover with lid and simmer for 2–3 minutes. Turn off heat and let sit for an additional 2 minutes. Serve immediately. Makes 1 large or 2 small servings.

Black Beans on Toast

This recipe can be made in less than 15 minutes and gives you a nice healthy dose of protein to jump-start your day. Also goes great over rice for lunch or dinner.

- 1 19-oz (540-mL) can black beans, drained and rinsed
- ½ tsp cumin
- ½ tsp salt
- ¼ tsp black pepper
- ¼ tsp garlic powder
- ¼ cup salsa
- ¼ cup vegetable stock
- 4 slices bread, toasted
- ½ cup vegan cheese, finely grated (optional)

In a medium pot on high heat, combine the beans, cumin, salt, pepper, garlic, salsa, and stock; and bring to a boil. Reduce heat and simmer for 8–10 minutes. Remove from heat and mash beans and serve over toast garnished with "cheese." Makes 2 large or 4 small servings.

Quick Muesli

You can put this recipe together before you leave on a trip.
—Ann, Canton, New York

- 4½ cups rolled oat flakes
- ½ cup wheat germ
- ½ cup wheat bran
- ½ cup oat bran
- 1 cup raisins
- ½ cup walnuts, roughly chopped
- ¼ cup raw sunflower seeds

In a large bowl, combine all ingredients and stir together until well mixed. Store in an airtight container. Makes approx. 8 cups.

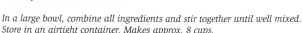

Eeny Meeny Chili Beany on Toast

Great for breakfast, lunch, or dinner. Serve over toast or a bun, topped with any of your favorite fixin's.

- 1 19-oz (540-mL) can beans (pinto or black), including liquid
- 1 3.8-oz (115-mL) can green chilies, chopped, including liquid
- ¼ cup ketchup
- 1 ½ tsp chili powder
- 1–2 tsp sugar
- ½ tsp onion powder
- ⅛ tsp garlic powder
- ¼ tsp salt
- ⅛ tsp crushed red pepper flakes
- 1 tsp Braggs or tamari
- 4 slices bread, toasted

In a medium pot on high heat, stir together the beans, chilies, ketchup, chili powder, sugar, onion powder, garlic powder, salt, red pepper flakes, and Braggs. Bring to a boil, then reduce heat to simmer, uncovered, for 10–15 minutes. Serve over toast. Makes 1 large or 2 small servings.

Salads & Dressings

PALE IS THE NEW TAN

Beth's Fresh & Fancy Raw-Slaw

This tasty recipe comes from the lovely Beth via the Internet. This salad is REALLY filling, and I actually enjoy it for breakfast as well as lunch and dinner! Sometimes, I will add a handful of chickpeas for extra protein. It's raw-tastic!

- 1 large carrot, grated
- 1 large apple, grated
- 1 cup sweet potatoes (or yams), grated
- ¼ cup raisins
- ¼ cup walnuts (or pecans), chopped
- 1–2 tbsp oil (e.g., flax or hemp)

In a medium bowl, combine all ingredients. Toss well and serve. Makes 2 large or 4 small servings.

Auntie Bonnie's Chickpea Salad

One of my favorite salad recipes. It can be made in five minutes flat, and is a good source of protein. It travels well in a container with a tight-fitting lid.

- 1 19-oz (540-mL) can chickpeas (garbanzo beans), drained and rinsed
- ¼ small red onion, minced
- 1–2 garlic cloves, minced
- 1 large tomato, diced
- ¼ cup fresh parsley, minced

- 3 tbsp oil (e.g., flax or hemp)
- 1 tbsp red wine vinegar
- 1 tsp lemon juice
- ¼ tsp salt
- ¼ tsp black pepper

In a large bowl, toss all ingredients together, and refrigerate for at least 1 hour before serving. Makes 2 large or 4 small servings.

Faux Egg Salad

This is the absolute BEST of the many faux egg recipes I have tried.
—Karen, Northwood, New Hampshire

- 1 lb (455 g) firm tofu
- ½ cup vegan mayonnaise (pg 181)
- 4 tbsp fresh parsley, chopped
- 1–2 pickles, diced, or ¼ cup relish
- 1½ tbsp prepared mustard
- 1–2 green onion stalks, chopped
- 2 celery stalks, diced
- 2 garlic cloves, minced
- 1½ tsp salt
- ¼ tsp turmeric

In a medium bowl, mash together all ingredients. Mix well and chill before serving. Makes 2 large or 4 small servings.

Claire's Red & Racy Potato Salad

I always found the generic potato salad very unappetizing, so I invented my own. It's a blend of sweet and spicy tastes, and always a hit at picnics. Now, I am passing it on to you so you too can be a potato salad diva.
—Claire, Los Angeles, California

- 20 small red potatoes, quartered
- ½ cup red onions, minced
- 1 cup seedless red grapes, sliced in half
- ¼ cup fresh cilantro, chopped
- ¼ cup vegan mayonnaise (pg 181)
- 3 tsp Dijon mustard
- ⅛ tsp black pepper

In a medium pot of water on high heat, boil potatoes just until tender. Drain and rinse potatoes under cold water, then set aside to cool. Once potatoes are cooled, combine them in a medium bowl with the remaining ingredients. Toss gently. Makes 2 large or 4 small servings.

Faux Chicken Salad

My favorite recipe for when I'm on-the-go or away from home.
—Adina, Trinidad, Colorado.

Serve over toast, as a side dish, as a sandwich filling, or alone. (For a variation, add 1–2 tsp of curry powder to spice it up a bit!). If you have trouble finding tempeh, you can use firm tofu, but it's not quite as effective.

- 1 cup tempeh, cubed
- ½ cup vegan mayonnaise (pg 181)
- 1 celery stalk, minced
- 1 medium dill pickle, minced
- ½ medium onion, chopped
- 2 tbsp fresh parsley, minced
- 2 tsp prepared mustard
- 2 tsp Braggs or tamari
- 1 garlic clove, minced

Steam the tempeh for 15 minutes on medium-high heat. Remove from heat and set aside to cool. In a medium bowl, combine the remaining ingredients with the tempeh and toss lightly. Makes 2 large or 4 small servings.

Fantastic Dijon Potato Salad

This delicate yet hardy salad is a perfect dish for any picnic or potluck.

- 14 small new potatoes, halved
- ⅓ cup red wine vinegar
- ¾ cup olive oil
- 2 tsp Dijon mustard
- 1 garlic clove, minced
- ⅛ tsp black pepper
- 2 tbsp fresh parsley, chopped
- 2 tbsp fresh dill, chopped
- 2 green onion stalks, chopped
- 1 medium red bell pepper, chopped

In a medium pot of water on high heat, boil potatoes just until tender. Drain and rinse potatoes under cold water, then set aside to cool. In a small bowl, whisk together the vinegar, oil, mustard, garlic, and pepper, and set aside. In a medium bowl, gently toss together the potatoes with the parsley, dill, green onion, bell pepper, and dressing. Makes 2 large or 4 small servings.

Rustic Quinoa & Yam Salad

In North America, yams are sometimes called sweet potatoes, and while they are similar, they are from a different plant species. If you're confused, ask your grocer and they'll point you in the right direction. If you can't find quinoa, a quick cooking rice like basmati will also do the trick. This recipe travels well in a container with a tight-fitting lid.

- 1 cup quinoa
- 2 cups water
- 1 medium onion, chopped
- 2 garlic cloves, minced
- 1½ cups yams, chopped
- 2 tbsp oil
- 1 medium red bell pepper, chopped
- 1 tsp cumin
- ¼ cup fresh cilantro, chopped
- 2 tbsp lemon juice
- 1 tbsp Braggs or tamari
- 1 tbsp maple syrup

In a medium saucepan, stir together the quinoa and water. Bring to a boil, then cover and reduce heat to medium-low. Simmer for 15 minutes or until cooked. Fluff with a fork and set aside to cool. In a large frying pan on medium heat, sauté the onion, garlic, and yams in oil until yams are tender but firm to the bite. Add the bell pepper and cumin and sauté for an additional 2 minutes. Set aside until cool. In a large bowl, combine the quinoa, yam mixture, cilantro, lemon juice, Braggs, and syrup. Mix well and chill before serving. Makes 4–6 servings.

Maple Dijon Dressing

*My absolute favorite thing from **LDV** are the salad dressings, this one in particular. I make it practically every week and pour it over whatever I'm eating. —Erica, mooshoes.com*

- ¼ cup olive oil
- ¼ cup oil (e.g., flax or hemp)
- ¼ cup red wine vinegar
- ⅓ cup maple syrup
- 1 tsp paprika
- 1 tsp celery seed
- ⅛ tsp salt
- 1 tsp Dijon mustard

In a jar or dressing bottle, combine all ingredients. Shake well before using. Makes approx. 1 cup.

Sweet Ginger Dressing

You MUST include this dressing in your new book. I tweaked it a bit so it is thicker and I use it as a dip for veggies. YUM!
—Natasha, Victoria, British Columbia

- ½ cup soft or medium tofu
- 2 tbsp gomashio (pg 189)
- 2 tbsp sesame oil
- ¼ cup oil (e.g., flax or hemp)
- ½ cup rice vinegar
- 2 tbsp maple syrup
- 1 tbsp miso
- 1 garlic clove
- 1½ tbsp fresh ginger, grated
- ½ tsp black pepper

With a blender or food processor, blend together all ingredients until smooth and creamy. Makes approx. 1½ cups.

Sarah & Tanya's You-Must-Make-This Dressing

Seriously. You must. You must make this dressing…. Go. Do it. Now!

- 1 green onion stalk, roughly chopped
- 1–2 garlic cloves
- 2 tbsp maple syrup
- 4 tbsp apple cider vinegar
- 1 tsp Dijon mustard
- 1 tsp fresh chives
- 1 tsp fresh dill
- 1 tsp fresh parsley
- ¼ cup olive oil
- ¼ cup oil (e.g., flax or hemp)
- ½ tsp salt

With a blender or food processor, blend all ingredients until smooth. Makes approx. ¾ cup.

Soups

BE PREPARED

Kathleen's Mom's Tortilla Chip Soup

I recently moved from NYC to Denmark with my wonderful Danish husband. I've found that this recipe works great because it's so easy, with ingredients you can find anywhere.... I even made it when staying in a tiny cottage in the middle of nowhere. —**Meagan, Copenhagen, Denmark**

- 1 small onion, chopped
- 1 tbsp oil
- 1 garlic clove, minced
- 1 small orange bell pepper, chopped
- 1 3.8-oz (115-mL) can green chilies, chopped, including liquid
- 2½ cups vegetable stock
- ¾ cup corn, fresh or frozen
- ½ cup fresh cilantro, chopped
- 1 19-oz (540-mL) can black beans, drained and rinsed
- ½ tsp chili powder
- ½ tsp dried basil
- ¼ tsp salt
- ¼ tsp black pepper
- 1 5.5-oz (156-mL) can tomato paste
- tortilla chips

In a medium saucepan on medium heat, sauté the onions in oil until translucent. Add the garlic, bell peppers, and chilies and sauté for 2–3 minutes. Add the stock, corn, cilantro, beans, chili powder, basil, salt, pepper, and tomato paste. Stir together well. Bring to a boil, then reduce heat. Cover with lid and simmer for 15–20 minutes. Place several tortilla chips in the bottom of each soup bowl before serving. Makes 2 large or 4 small servings.

Go-Go Gadget Green Soup

A raw-tastic soup! If you can't find hemp seeds, try raw cashews instead.

- 2 cups spinach, tightly packed
- ½ cup fresh parsley
- ¼ cup shelled hemp seeds
- ½ tsp salt
- ½ tbsp fresh ginger, grated
- 1 tbsp oil (e.g., flax or hemp)
- 2 tbsp walnuts
- 2 cups water
- 1 avocado, diced
- 1 large carrot, finely grated

With a blender or food processor, blend the spinach, parsley, hemp seeds, salt, ginger, oil, walnuts, and water until smooth. Portion into bowls and garnish each with equal amounts of avocado and carrot. Serve immediately. Makes 2 large or 4 small servings.

Home-Style Green Pea Soup

Nothing gives you the creature comfort feeling of home more that a beautiful bowl of soup

- 1 medium onion, chopped
- 2 garlic cloves, minced
- 1 tbsp oil
- 2 medium potatoes, chopped
- 1 medium carrot, chopped
- 4 cups vegetable stock
- 1 cup dry green split peas
- 1 tbsp Braggs or tamari
- 1 tsp dried oregano
- ½ tsp cumin
- ⅛ tsp black pepper
- ⅛ tsp salt

In a large soup pot on medium heat, sauté the onions and garlic in the oil until onions are translucent. Add the potatoes, carrots, stock, peas, Braggs, oregano, cumin, pepper, and salt. Stir to combine. Bring to a boil, then reduce heat to medium-low. Simmer for 25–30 minutes or until peas are cooked. With a blender or food processor, blend half or all of the soup until smooth (be careful when blending hot liquids); return to pot and reheat. Makes 4 servings.

Vanessa's Lentil-Quinoa Stew

This recipe is possibly my favorite thing in the entire world. It is so simple, easy to prepare, and the end result is so delicious. I make it regularly, and I even passed the recipe on to my omnivore momma who absolutely loved it as well. —Caroline, Eugene, Oregon

- 1 small onion, chopped
- 1 tbsp oil
- 1 celery stalk, diced
- 1 small carrot, chopped
- 1 garlic clove, minced
- 2½ cups vegetable stock
- ½ cup dry red lentils
- ¼ cup quinoa
- ½ tsp dried basil
- ½ tsp dried oregano
- ½ tsp salt
- ½ tsp black pepper
- 1 medium tomato, diced
- ¼ cup fresh cilantro, minced
- 1 tbsp apple cider vinegar

In a medium soup pot on medium heat, sauté the onion in oil until translucent. Add the celery, carrot, and garlic and sauté for 5 minutes. Add the stock, lentils, quinoa, basil, oregano, salt, and pepper. Bring to a boil, then reduce heat. Cover with lid and simmer for 20–25 minutes or until the lentils are tender. With a blender or food processor, blend half or all of the soup until smooth (be careful when blending hot liquids); return to pot and stir in the tomato, cilantro, and vinegar. Reheat and serve. Makes 2 large or 4 small servings.

Tanya's Curried Squash Soup

A scrumptious creation that is always a hit at potlucks.

- 1 small onion, chopped
- 1 tbsp oil
- 1½ cups cauliflower, chopped
- 1 cup yams, chopped
- 1 cup squash (e.g., butternut, acorn, or buttercup), chopped
- 1 small potato, chopped
- 1 small leek, sliced (white and pale green parts only)
- 1 cup vegetable stock
- 1 14-oz (398-mL) can coconut milk
- 1½ tsp curry powder
- ½ tsp turmeric
- 2 tsp Braggs or tamari

*In a large soup pot on medium heat, sauté the onion
in the oil until translucent. Add the cauliflower, yam,
squash, potato, and leek and simmer for an additional 3
minutes. Add the stock, coconut milk, curry, turmeric, and
Braggs. Bring to a boil, then reduce heat to low. Simmer
for 10–15 minutes or until vegetables are cooked. With a
blender or food processor, blend half or all of the soup until
smooth (be careful when blending hot liquids); return to pot and reheat.
Makes 2 large or 4 small servings.*

Roasted Carrot Coconut Soup

This is so delicious and makes the house smell amazing.
—Sheila, Lake Country, British Columbia

- 5–6 large carrots, diced
- 1 small onion, chopped
- 1 garlic clove, minced
- 1 tsp fresh ginger, grated
- 1 stick fresh lemongrass (tough outer layers removed), chopped (use bottom 6 in only)
- ½ tsp garam masala (pg 189)
- ½ tsp ground coriander seeds
- 2 tbsp oil
- 1 cup vegetable stock
- 1 14-oz (398-mL) can coconut milk
- 1 tbsp lime juice
- ¼ cup fresh cilantro, chopped
- ½ tsp salt
- ¼ tsp black pepper

Preheat oven to 400°F (205°C). In a medium baking dish, combine the carrots, onion, garlic, ginger, lemongrass, garam masala, coriander, and oil until well coated. Bake for 35–40 minutes, or until carrots are tender. Just before vegetables are done, in a medium soup pot, bring the stock to a boil. Reduce heat, add the roasted vegetables, and simmer for 2–3 minutes. Add the coconut milk. With a blender or food processor, blend half or all of the soup until smooth (be careful when blending hot liquids); return to pot and stir in the lime juice, cilantro, salt, and pepper. Reheat and serve. Makes 2 large or 4 small servings.

Cauliflower Red Lentil Soup

So easy and delicious! —**Auntie Bonnie, Victoria, British Columbia**

- 1 medium onion, chopped
- 1 tbsp oil
- 1 tbsp fresh ginger, grated
- 4 garlic cloves, minced
- 1 tsp cumin seeds
- ½ tsp red pepper flakes
- 1 tsp turmeric
- 2½ cups vegetable stock
- 2 cups cauliflower, cut into bite-sized pieces
- 2 medium tomatoes, chopped
- 1 cup dry red lentils
- ¼ cup fresh cilantro, minced
- ½ tsp salt

In a medium soup pot on medium heat, sauté the onion in the oil until translucent. Add the ginger, garlic, cumin, red pepper flakes, and turmeric and sauté for 2 minutes; stir constantly to avoid sticking. Add the stock, cauliflower, tomatoes, and lentils. Bring to a boil, then reduce heat. Cover with lid and simmer for 15–20 minutes or until veggies and lentils are cooked. Stir in the cilantro and salt, remove from heat, and let sit 5 minutes before serving. Makes 2 large or 4 small servings.

Quick Carrot Ginger Soup

This is my favorite. Especially when I'm not feeling well.... Gives me extra vitamins to get better. —Emma via MySpace

- 1 small onion, chopped
- 1 tbsp oil
- 1 small potato, cubed
- 2 large carrots, chopped
- 2 tsp fresh ginger, grated
- 2 cups vegetable stock
- ¼ tsp salt
- ½ tsp black pepper

In a medium soup pot on medium heat, sauté the onion in the oil until translucent. Add the potato, carrots, and ginger and sauté for 2–3 minutes; stir constantly to avoid sticking. Add the stock, salt, and pepper. Bring to a boil, then reduce heat. Simmer for 15–20 minutes, or until the vegetables are tender. With a blender or food processor, blend half or all the soup until smooth (be careful when blending hot liquids); return to pot, reheat, and serve. Makes 2 large or 4 small servings.

Mulligatawny Soup

The page for this recipe in HIAV is yellow from curry powder but thankfully I can still read the recipe. This soup made my husband never want to eat soup with meat in it again! It proved to him that meat is NOT what gives flavor to food. —**Paisley, Central Point, Oregon**

- 1 large onion, chopped
- 3 celery stalks, chopped
- 3 tbsp oil
- ½ tsp cayenne pepper
- 1 tsp turmeric
- 1 tsp ground coriander seeds
- 1 tsp curry powder
- 2 tbsp Braggs or tamari
- 6 cups vegetable stock or water
- 2 medium carrots, chopped
- 2 large potatoes, cubed
- ½ cup rice
- 1 small red bell pepper, chopped
- 1 small green bell pepper, chopped
- 1 small tomato, chopped
- 1 cup cauliflower, chopped
- ¾ cup unsweetened coconut, grated
- 1 tbsp lemon juice
- 1 tbsp fresh cilantro (optional)

In a large soup pot on medium heat, sauté the onions and celery in the oil until onions are translucent. Add the cayenne, turmeric, coriander, curry, Braggs, stock, carrots, potatoes, and rice. Bring to a boil and reduce heat. Let simmer for 15–20 minutes. Add the bell peppers, tomato, cauliflower, coconut, lemon juice, and cilantro. Stir together and simmer 5–10 more minutes until vegetables are tender and rice is cooked. With a blender or food processor, blend half or all of the soup until smooth (be careful when blending hot liquids); return to pot and reheat. Makes 4 large servings.

On Golden Pond Mushroom Soup

LDV was the first cookbook that made vegan cooking seem possible. Without it I would most likely still be vegetarian. This recipe is really easy to make and I always look forward to bringing the leftovers to work the next day. —Lauren, Farmington Valley, Connecticut

- 1 small onion, chopped
- 8–10 large mushrooms, chopped
- 2 tbsp oil
- 2 tbsp Braggs or tamari
- 1–2 tsp paprika
- 1 tsp dried dill
- ½ tsp salt
- ½ tsp black pepper
- 2 tbsp flour
- 1 cup vegetable stock
- 1½ cups vegan milk

In a medium soup pot on medium heat, sauté the onions and mushrooms in the oil until onions are translucent. Add the Braggs, paprika, dill, salt, and pepper, and sauté for an additional 5 minutes; stir often to avoid sticking. Stir in the flour to create a mushroom paste. Slowly add the stock ½ cup at a time, stirring often as it thickens. Add the "milk" and let simmer for 8–10 minutes before serving. Makes 2 large or 4 small servings.

Bodacious Bean & Barley Soup

After I made this soup for the first time, I wrote beside the recipe: "I think this soup is the best soup I've ever had." Needless to say, I went on to make it for everyone I know and gave the recipe to all of them.
—Erin, Vancouver, British Columbia

- 1 small onion, chopped
- 6 garlic cloves, minced
- 2 tbsp oil
- ⅔ cup pearl barley
- 3½ cups vegetable stock
- 1 cup canned chickpeas (garbanzo beans), drained and rinsed
- 1 tsp cumin
- 1 tsp turmeric
- 1 cup soy yogurt
- ½ cup fresh cilantro, chopped
- 1 tsp dried mint (or 1 tbsp fresh)
- ⅛ tsp salt
- ⅛ tsp black pepper

In a large soup pot on medium heat, sauté the onions and garlic in the oil until onions are translucent. Add the barley and sauté for an additional minute. Add the stock, chickpeas, cumin, and turmeric. Bring to a boil, then reduce heat to medium-low. Simmer for about 45 minutes, or until barley is tender. Stir in yogurt, cilantro, mint, salt, and pepper. Remove from heat and let sit for 5 minutes before serving. Makes 2 large or 4 small servings.

Delightful Broccoli & Red Pepper Soup

My friends and family like to get together for dinner as often as possible to catch up on things. Being the only vegan, I'm encouraged to make something vegan to add to the dinner. The garlic spread on bread [pg 83] and this soup have always been hits. In fact, I now get requests for the soup; it is now just referred to as "The Soup." —Lori, Windsor, Ontario

- 1 medium onion, chopped
- 2 garlic cloves, chopped
- 1 tbsp oil
- 4 cups broccoli, chopped
- 1 medium red bell pepper, chopped
- 3–4 cups vegetable stock
- 1 tsp Braggs or tamari
- ½ tsp dried tarragon
- ¼ tsp dried thyme
- ⅛ tsp black pepper

In a large soup pot on medium heat, sauté the onion and garlic in the oil until onions are translucent. Add the broccoli, bell pepper, stock, Braggs, tarragon, thyme, and black pepper. Bring to a boil, then reduce heat to medium-low. Simmer for 15 minutes or until vegetables are tender. With a blender or food processor, blend half or all of the soup until smooth (be careful when blending hot liquids); return to pot and reheat. Makes 4 servings.

Quick Miso Soup for One

Miso can be found in Japanese markets and health food stores and comes in a wide variety of flavors. Some are nuttier than others. You really can't go wrong with the one you choose; they're all delicious and highly nutritious. Remember that cooking miso will destroy its healthy attributes, so avoid boiling your miso by stirring it into your dish in the last few minutes.

- 2 cups water
- 1 garlic clove, peeled and slightly crushed
- 1 in (2½ cm) fresh ginger, roughly chopped
- 2 tbsp miso
- ¼ cup firm or extra firm tofu, cubed
- 1 small carrot, grated or finely chopped
- ¼ cup green veggies of your choice
  (e.g., bok choy, baby spinach, peas, kale), finely chopped

In a medium soup pot on high heat, bring water to a boil. Reduce heat and add the garlic and ginger. Cover with lid and let simmer for 6–8 minutes. Remove garlic and ginger with a slotted spoon and turn off heat. In a small bowl, stir together the miso and 3 tablespoons of the hot soup stock as prepared above. Stir until the miso is smooth. Add this and the tofu, carrots, and green veggies to the pot. Cover with a lid and let sit for 3–5 minutes before serving. Makes 1 large serving.

Raunchy Red Lentil Soup

This warm, thick soup can be served with basmati rice or chapati or other flatbread.

- 1 large onion, chopped
- 1 tbsp oil
- 3 garlic cloves, minced
- 1 jalapeño, seeded and minced
- 3 cups vegetable stock
- 1 cup dry red lentils
- 1 tsp turmeric
- 1½ tsp cumin
- ½ tsp salt
- 1 tsp fresh ginger, finely grated
- 2 small tomatoes, chopped
- ¼ cup fresh cilantro, chopped

In a medium soup pot on medium heat, sauté the onion in the oil until translucent. Add the garlic and jalapeño, and sauté for an additional 5 minutes. Add the stock, lentils, turmeric, cumin, salt, and ginger. Bring to a boil, then reduce heat. Cover with lid and simmer for 15 minutes or until the lentils are tender. With a blender or food processor, blend half or all of the soup until smooth (be careful when blending hot liquids); return to pot and stir in tomatoes and cilantro. Cover with lid, remove from heat, and let stand 2–3 minutes before serving. Makes 2 large or 4 small servings.

Margo's Veggie Peanut Stew

I love, love, love this recipe. Plus, you can get ingredients at the corner store.

- 1 large onion, chopped
- 1 tbsp oil
- 1 large carrot, chopped
- ½ tsp fresh ginger, grated
- ½ tsp salt
- ¼ tsp cayenne pepper
- 1 large sweet potato, chopped
- 1½ cups vegetable stock
- ⅓ cup peanut butter
- 1 cup tomato juice
- ⅓ cup roasted peanuts

In a medium soup pot on medium heat, sauté the onion in the oil until translucent. Add the carrot, ginger, salt, and cayenne and sauté for 5 minutes. Add the sweet potato and stock and bring to a boil, then reduce heat. Cover with lid and simmer for 10–15 minutes, or until vegetables are tender. Stir in the peanut butter and tomato juice. With a blender or food processor, blend half or all of the soup until smooth (be careful when blending hot liquids); return to pot and reheat. Serve garnished with roasted peanuts. Makes 2 large or 4 small servings.

Adam's Yellow Split Pea Chowder

This wonderful recipe came via email from Adam in Red Deer, Alberta.

- 1 small onion, chopped
- 2 medium carrots, chopped
- 2 celery stalks, chopped
- 1 tbsp oil
- 3 cups vegetable stock
- ¼ cup brown rice
- ¼ cup dry yellow split peas
- ½ tsp dried basil
- ½ tsp salt

In a medium soup pot on medium heat, sauté the onions, carrots, and celery in the oil until onions are translucent. Add the remaining ingredients. Bring to a boil, then reduce heat. Cover with lid and simmer for 45 minutes or until rice and peas are cooked. With a blender or food processor, blend half or all of the soup until smooth (be careful when blending hot liquids); return to pot, reheat, and serve. Makes 2 large or 4 small servings.

Hungry Person Stew

This politically correct stew from *GOV* is as chunky as it is meaty, but in an animal-friendly sort of way. Seitan (wheat gluten) has a firm and meat-like texture that reminds us we don't have to be cruel to be kind.

- 1 small onion, chopped
- 5 medium mushrooms, chopped
- 1 tbsp oil
- 2 medium carrots, chopped
- 1 large potato, chopped
- 2 cups vegetable stock
- ½ tsp dried thyme
- ¼ tsp red pepper flakes
- ⅛ tsp black pepper
- 1 5.5-oz (156-mL) can tomato paste
- 1 cup seitan (pg 186-187), chopped
- 1 cup fresh or frozen peas

In a large soup pot on medium heat, sauté the onions and mushrooms in the oil until onions are translucent. Add the carrots and sauté for an additional minute. Add the potato, stock, thyme, red pepper flakes, black pepper, and tomato paste. Bring to a boil, then reduce heat to low. Simmer for 15 minutes or until potatoes are cooked. Turn off heat and stir in the seitan and peas. Let stand for 5 minutes before serving. Makes 2 large or 4 small servings.

Hearty Winter Potato Soup

**Potatoes are highly nutritious, an excellent source of vits B and C.
This soup is most excellent for that winter funk.**

* 1 medium onion, chopped
* 3 garlic cloves, chopped
* 4–6 mushrooms, chopped
* 2 tbsp oil
* 4–5 medium potatoes, cubed
* 3 cups vegetable stock or water
* 1 red bell pepper, chopped
* ⅛ tsp red pepper flakes
* ½ tsp ground coriander seeds
* 1 tsp cumin
* 1 tsp dried basil
* ½ tsp salt
* ¼ tsp black pepper
* 2 tsp Braggs or tamari
* 1 cup vegan milk
* 2 green onion stalks, sliced (for garnish)
* croutons (for garnish)

*In a large soup pot, sauté the onion, garlic, and mushrooms in the oil until
onions are translucent. Add the potatoes, stock, bell pepper, red pepper flakes,
coriander, cumin, basil, salt, black pepper, and Braggs. Bring to a boil, then
reduce heat to low. Simmer for 10–20 minutes until potatoes are tender.
Add "milk." With a blender or food processor, blend half or all of the soup
until smooth (be careful when blending hot liquids); return to pot, reheat,
and serve. Garnish with green onions and serve with croutons. Makes 4–6
servings.*

Microwave Curried Chickpea Potato Soup

Who knew you could make such good soup in a microwave?

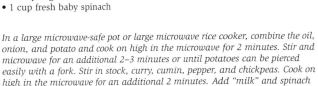

- 1 tbsp oil
- 1 small onion, chopped
- 1 large potato, chopped
- 1 cup vegetable stock
- 2 tsp curry powder
- ½ tsp cumin
- ⅛ tsp black pepper
- 1 19-oz (540-mL) can chickpeas (garbanzo beans), drained and rinsed
- ½ cup vegan milk
- 1 cup fresh baby spinach

In a large microwave-safe pot or large microwave rice cooker, combine the oil, onion, and potato and cook on high in the microwave for 2 minutes. Stir and microwave for an additional 2–3 minutes or until potatoes can be pierced easily with a fork. Stir in stock, curry, cumin, pepper, and chickpeas. Cook on high in the microwave for an additional 2 minutes. Add "milk" and spinach and stir. Let sit for 1 minute before serving. Makes 2 servings.

Microwave Voluptuous Vegetable Soup

You can add any veggies you want to this recipe. The more the merrier!

- 1 tbsp oil
- 1 small onion, chopped
- 1 celery stalk, chopped
- 4 mushrooms, chopped
- ½ cup broccoli, chopped
- ½ cup zucchini, chopped
- ½ cup red bell pepper, chopped
- 1 large tomato, chopped
- ¾ cup water
- 1 tsp dried basil
- 1 tsp dried oregano
- ½ tsp black pepper
- ½ tsp salt
- 1 19-oz (540-mL) can beans (e.g., pinto or black), drained and rinsed

In a large microwave-safe pot or large microwave rice cooker, combine the oil, onion, celery, mushrooms, and broccoli and cook on high in the microwave for 4 minutes. Stir and add the zucchini, bell pepper, and tomato. Microwave on high for an additional 4 minutes. Stir in the remaining ingredients. Microwave on high for an additional 4 minutes. Makes 2 servings.

Sarah's Hot & Sour Ginger Soup

All these ingredients can be found in Chinatown. Yum!

- 3 tbsp fresh ginger, grated
- ½ cup shiitake or oyster mushrooms, chopped
- 1 ½ tbsp dark sesame oil
- 4 cups vegetable stock
- rice noodles or noodles of your choice
  (e.g., udon or buckwheat) (enough for 4 servings)
- ½ tsp red pepper flakes
- 3 tbsp rice vinegar
- 1 tbsp Braggs or tamari
- ½ lb (225 g) firm tofu, cubed
- 20 snow peas, ends removed

In a large soup pot on medium-low heat, sauté the ginger and mushrooms in the oil for 1–2 minutes, stirring often to prevent burning. Add the stock, noodles, and red pepper flakes. Bring to a boil, then reduce heat to medium-low. Simmer for 3–5 minutes or until noodles are cooked. Turn off heat, add vinegar, Braggs, tofu, and snow peas. Cover and let stand for 5 minutes before serving. Makes 4 large servings.

Dips & Spreads

ASK FOR DIRECTION

Olivada

A multi-purpose spread that you can serve with crackers, bread, as a sandwich spread or pizza sauce, or toss it into hot noodles.

- 1 cup olives, pitted
- ⅓ cup oil (e.g., olive, flax, or hemp)
- 1–2 garlic cloves, minced
- ⅛ tsp black pepper

With a blender or food processor, blend all the ingredients until it becomes a coarse paste. Makes approx. ¾ cup.

Gillian's Lentil Dip

Serve with flatbread or crackers ... and try your best not to eat it all before your guests arrive.

- 1 cup dry red lentils
- 1½ cups water
- 2 tbsp olive oil
- 3 tbsp oil (e.g., flax, hemp, or grapeseed)
- ¼ cup lemon juice
- 1–2 garlic cloves
- 1 tsp cumin
- ¼ tsp salt

In a medium pot, bring water and lentils to a boil. Reduce heat and simmer for 2–3 minutes. Remove from heat, cover, and let stand for 12–15 minutes. In a food processor, blend the lentils, oils, lemon juice, garlic, cumin, and salt until smooth. Makes approx. 2 cups.

Walnut Chickpea Hummus

This recipe is great for when you're stuck somewhere and can't find tahini. This is also a fantastic sandwich spread (pg 87-88) or can be served with pita.

- 1 19-oz (540-mL) can chickpeas (garbanzo beans), drained and rinsed
- 1 cup walnuts
- 5–10 olives
- 1–2 garlic cloves
- ¼ cup fresh basil, tightly packed
- 1 small tomato, roughly chopped
- 2 tbsp oil (e.g., flax or hemp)
- 2 tbsp water
- ½ tsp salt
- ¼ tsp black pepper

In a food processor, combine all ingredients and blend until smooth. Makes approx. 2 cups.

Avocado Tomato Salsa

A delicious and lightning fast salsa! Serve with tortilla chips.

- 1 medium tomato, chopped
- 1 avocado, peeled, pit removed, and cubed
- ¼ cup fresh cilantro, minced
- 1 green onion stalk, minced
- 1 tbsp oil (e.g., flax or hemp)
- 2 tsp lime juice

In a medium bowl, stir together all ingredients. Makes approx. 2 cups.

Edamame Hummus

I love eating this with fresh vegetables.
—Auntie Bonnie, Victoria, British Columbia.

This is a wonderful multi-purpose spread that you can serve with crackers, bread, veggies, or even as a sandwich spread. Edamame is high in protein and will keep your energy up while you schlep your luggage across the country.

- ¾ cup frozen edamame beans, pre-shucked
- 2 cups fresh spinach, tightly packed
- 2–3 garlic cloves
- ½ cup tahini
- 2 tbsp olive oil
- 2 tbsp oil (e.g., flax or hemp)
- 1 tbsp lemon juice
- 1 tbsp Braggs or tamari
- 1–2 tsp Asian chili-garlic sauce (or other hot sauce)
- ½ tsp salt
- ¼ tsp black pepper

Steam edamame until bright green and thawed. In a food processor, combine the edamame and remaining ingredients, and blend until smooth. Makes approx. 2 cups.

Sunflower Seed Avocado Spread

This rich multi-purpose spread is delicious, nutritious, and a snap to make. Fantastic on sandwiches or crackers or stuffed into a red bell pepper (pg 87).

- ½ cup raw sunflower seeds
- ¼ cup vegan milk
- ¼ cup tahini
- 1 avocado
- 1 tsp lemon juice
- ½ tsp turmeric
- ¼ tsp mustard seeds
- ½ tsp black pepper
- ¼ tsp salt

In a food processor, blend all ingredients until smooth and thick. Will keep in a sealable container in the fridge for 4–7 days. Makes approx. 1 cup.

Dips

Garlic Spread

I know this recipe off by heart now. It's my fav. —Lori, Windsor, Ontario.

For garlic toast, spread this over bread slices, wrap bread in foil, and
bake at 350°F (175°C) for 15–25 minutes.

- 6–10 garlic cloves, minced
- ½ small onion, minced
- ⅛ tsp salt
- ½ cup olive oil

*With a blender or food processor, blend all ingredients, drizzling in oil
gradually, until smooth. Makes approx. ¾ cup.*

Sun-Dried Tomato "Butter"

A fun and easy way to jazz up your vegan margarine.
Now everyone show me your best "jazz hands"!

- ½ cup vegan margarine
- 2 tbsp fresh parsley
- 1 garlic clove
- 4–6 sun-dried tomatoes
- ¼ tsp salt
- ¼ tsp black pepper

*With a blender or food processor, blend all ingredients
until smooth. Spoon into a small serving dish and
refrigerate for 1 hour before serving. Makes approx. ½ cup.*

Chive "Butter"

It's not easy being green, but it sure is delicious.

- ½ cup vegan margarine
- ¼ cup (tightly packed) fresh chives
- 1–2 tsp oil (e.g, flax or hemp)

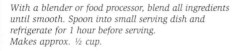

With a blender or food processor, blend all ingredients until smooth. Spoon into small serving dish and refrigerate for 1 hour before serving.
Makes approx. ½ cup.

Easy Veggie "Butter"

This recipe is so easy to prepare; it's great on toast, muffins, whatevah.

- ¾ cup soft tofu
- 2 tbsp oil (e.g., flax or hemp)
- ⅛ tsp salt
- ⅛ tsp turmeric

With a blender or food processor, blend all the ingredients until well mixed. Will keep in a sealable container in the fridge for 4–7 days. Makes approx. 1 cup.

Aloo-Yoop Curry Potato Wrap

This wonderful recipe comes from Sara in Paris, Ontario! To add a little pizzazz, spread a little hummus (pg 80-81) on the wrap before you add the potatoes. Wrap them up tightly in plastic wrap and they travel well for picnics, road trips, or a day at the beach.

- 1 small onion, minced
- 1 tbsp oil
- 2 medium potatoes, diced (approx. 2 cups)
- 2 medium sweet potatoes, diced (approx. 2 cups)
- 1 cup canned chickpeas (garbanzo beans), drained and rinsed
- 1 tsp cumin
- ½ tsp curry powder
- ¼ tsp cayenne pepper
- ¼ tsp salt
- ¼ tsp black pepper
- 1 14-oz (398-mL) can coconut milk
- ¼ cup vegetable stock
- ¼ cup peas, frozen or fresh
- 4 large tortillas (or other flatbread)

In a large saucepan on medium heat, sauté the onion in the oil until translucent. Add the potatoes, yams, chickpeas, cumin, curry, cayenne, salt, pepper, coconut milk, and stock and bring to a boil. Reduce heat and let simmer (without lid) for 15–20 minutes or until potatoes are cooked, stirring occasionally to prevent sticking. Once potatoes are ready and liquid is reduced, stir in peas, cover with lid, and let sit 5 minutes. Set out tortillas and spoon equal portions of the potato mixture onto each. Wrap and serve. Makes 4 wraps.

Red Pepper "Sandwich"

While this is not technically a sandwich, I do like to take it with me on trips as an alternative to eating bread—sometimes when you travel, the last thing you need is more gluten gumming up the works. Ya dig?
Fill your red bell pepper with this or any other spread, like hummus (pg 80-81), or leftovers. Wrap tightly in plastic wrap and then again in tin foil to keep your "sandwich" chilled in your bag.

- 2 large red bell peppers
- 1 cup cooked rice (or other grain)
- ¾ cup canned beans of your choice, drained and rinsed
- 1 medium tomato, roughly chopped
- ¼ cup olives of your choice
- ¼ cup fresh parsley
- 2 tbsp oil (e.g., flax or hemp)
- 2 tbsp walnuts
- ½ tsp salt
- ¼ tsp black pepper

Carefully slice the bell peppers in half, removing the seeds and stems. Set aside. With a blender or food processor, pulse together the remaining ingredients. Spoon equal portions of mixture into each pepper half. Makes 2 large or 4 small servings.

Burgers, Sandwiches & Wraps

Entrées

Rice Paper Veggie Wraps

Light, refreshing, and easy to make. Excellent for picnics or hot summer days when cooking seems impossible

- 4–6 mushrooms, chopped
- ½ cup Braggs or tamari
- 1 large carrot, grated
- 4 radishes, grated
- 1½ cups cabbage, grated
- 2 green onion stalks, chopped
- 1 medium tomato, chopped
- 1 cup sunflower sprouts (or other sprouts)
- ½ cup hummus (pg 80-81)
- 6 sheets of rice paper

In a small bowl, marinate the mushrooms in the Braggs for 10–15 minutes. (While marinating, you can prepare the remaining vegetables and set aside.) Fill a large bowl with lukewarm water and soak 1 sheet of rice paper until it becomes soft and pliable. Shake carefully or pat off excess water. Lay the sheet down on a plate or cutting board and fill the center with a little bit of each vegetable, including the mushrooms and sprouts, and about 2 tablespoons of hummus. Wrap up like a burrito and lay, seam-side down, on plate. Repeat process with remaining ingredients. Use the leftover marinade as a dip. Makes 6 wraps.

Sarah's Stranded-in-the-Middle-of-Nowhere Sandwich

This very simple recipe has saved my life too many times to count because the ingredients are readily available just about everywhere. It may seem that the restaurant, café, or truck stop doesn't have anything on the menu for you, but it will probably have these ingredients on hand. Just smile at your server and ask ... don't forget to tip well if they go out of their way to help.

- 4 slices of bread
- 1 avocado
- 1 red bell pepper, sliced
- cucumber slices
- sprouts or lettuce leaves
- black pepper (to taste)
- salt (to taste)

Lay out slices of bread. Cut avocado in half and remove pit. Carefully slice avocado flesh vertically and then horizontally, then scoop out flesh and spread even amounts of avocado on bread slices, like you would with margarine. On 2 slices of bread, layer equal amounts of veggies, and salt and pepper to taste. Top with remaining bread slices. Makes 2 sandwiches.

Spicy Black Bean Burgers

A tasty favorite to make and bring to work for lunch the next day.
—Melissa, New York City

- ½ cup flour
- 1 small onion, diced
- 2 garlic cloves, minced
- ½ tsp dried oregano
- 1 small hot chili pepper or jalapeño, minced
- 1 tbsp oil
- ½ medium red bell pepper, diced
- 1 19-oz (540-mL) can black beans, drained and rinsed
- ½ cup corn niblets
- ½ cup bread crumbs
- ¼ tsp cumin
- ½ tsp salt
- 2 tsp chili powder
- 2 tbsp fresh parsley, minced (optional)

On a small plate, set aside flour for coating. In a medium saucepan on medium-high heat, sauté the onions, garlic, oregano, and chili pepper in the oil until onions are translucent. Add the bell pepper and sauté another 2 minutes, until pepper is tender. Set aside. In a large bowl, mash the beans. Stir in the onion-pepper mixture and remaining ingredients. Mix well. Divide and shape mixture into 4, 5, or 6 patties. Lay down each patty in flour, coating each side. Cook in a lightly oiled frying pan on medium-high heat for 5–10 minutes or until browned on both sides. Makes 4 large or 5–6 small patties.

Big Ben's Lentil Burgers

These are so delicious and simple to make. I add a small can of chopped green chilies to the mix and it spices it up just enough. I make them a couple times a month and have even served them on Thanksgiving.
—Steve, Phoenix, Arizona.

Serve like a regular burger—an all-vegan patty, special sauce, lettuce, vegan cheese, pickles, and onions on a sesame bun!

- ¾ cup wheat germ
- 1 19-oz (540-mL) can lentils, drained, rinsed, and mashed
- 1 cup bread crumbs
- ¼ cup onions, chopped
- 3 tbsp oil
- ½ tsp salt
- ½ tsp black pepper

On a small plate, set aside 2 tablespoons of the wheat germ for coating. In a medium bowl, with your hands, mash together the remaining wheat germ with the remaining ingredients. Divide and shape into 4 patties. Lay down each patty in wheat germ, coating each side. Cook in a lightly oiled frying pan on medium-high heat for 5–10 minutes, flipping occasionally. Makes 4 patties.

Black Bean & Sweet Potato Burritos

This recipe takes a few more minutes then a lot of the recipes in this book but, man, is it worth the time. Wrap these suckers up tightly in plastic wrap and they make great travel companions.

- 2 medium sweet potatoes, diced (approx. 4 cups)
- 1 small onion, chopped
- 1 tbsp oil
- 1 19-oz (540-mL) can black beans, drained and rinsed
- 1 cup vegetable stock
- 2 garlic cloves, minced
- 1½ tbsp chili powder
- 2 tsp ground mustard
- 1 tsp cumin
- ½ tsp salt
- 4 large flour tortillas
- ¼ cup salsa
- 1 cup vegan cheese, grated (optional)

In a large pot of salted water, boil the sweet potatoes. While they are cooking, in a medium saucepan on medium heat, sauté the onion in the oil until translucent. Add the beans, stock, garlic, chili powder, mustard, cumin, and salt. Increase heat to medium-high and simmer, uncovered, for 15 minutes. Drain water from sweet potatoes, then return them to pot and mash. Set aside. Once bean mixture is done, mash and set aside. Spread onto each tortilla: 1 tbsp salsa, ¼ of the sweet potatoes, ¼ of the beans, and ¼ of the "cheese." Roll up each burrito and serve as is, or bake in oven until crisp. Makes 4 burritos.

Burnin' Butt Burritos

As silly as it sounds, I never would have thought to add something like broccoli to a burrito, but it absolutely makes the burrito. I like to roast the veggies with garlic in the oven before I add them to the burrito.
—Candyce, Nashville, Tennessee.

- ½ small onion, chopped
- 2 garlic cloves, minced
- ½ cup broccoli, chopped
- 4 mushrooms, chopped
- ½ medium red bell pepper, chopped
- 1–3 jalapeño peppers, seeded and minced
- 2 tbsp oil
- 4 large flour tortillas
- refried beans (see pg 132)
- vegan cheese (optional)
- salsa
- 2 cups cooked rice

Preheat oven to 350°F (175°C). In a medium saucepan, sauté the onions, garlic, broccoli, mushrooms, peppers, and jalapeños in the oil on medium-high heat until onions are translucent. Set aside. Spread onto each tortilla a thin layer of refried beans, "cheese," salsa, rice, and the veggie mixture. Roll up each burrito and lay on cookie sheet. Bake for 15–20 minutes. Makes 4 burritos.

Zucchini Pasta

Have you searched through your parents' pantry and all you can find is white food? White pasta, white bread, white rice? All that bleached-out food must be tying your colon into a knot. Why not go raw! I like to add ¼ cup chickpeas to give a little extra weight to my meal. This easy fresh recipe can be made in a matter of minutes.

• 2 zucchinis

Using a grater or vegetable peeler, grate or peel the zucchini into long, thin strips. Toss zucchini with Fresh Five-Minute Basil Tomato Sauce (pg 123), Tyler & Phoebe's Perfect Pesto Sauce (pg 122), or Fettuccini Alfredo sauce (pg 95). Makes 2 servings.

Fettuccini Alfredo

Easy. Cheezy. Beautiful. This wonderful *no-cook* sauce can also be tossed with Zucchini Pasta (pg 94).

- fettuccini pasta, enough for 2 people
- ¾ cup raw cashews
- ¼ cup raw pine nuts
- 1 tbsp lemon juice
- 1 garlic clove
- 2 tsp nutritional yeast
- ½ tsp ground thyme
- ½ tsp salt
- ¾ tsp black pepper
- ¾ cup water

In a large pot of salted water, boil the pasta. While pasta is cooking, with a blender or food processor, blend the remaining ingredients until smooth. When pasta is cooked, drain noodles and return to pot. Add the sauce to the noodles and toss well. Serve immediately. Makes 2 large or 4 small servings.

Peanut Butter Pasta

My absolute fav is the Peanut Butter Pasta from GOV. *I add diced extra-firm tofu as well.* —**Carol, Bourbonnais, Illinois**

- pasta, enough for 2 people
- ⅓ cup peanut butter
- ¼ cup hot water
- 1 tbsp Braggs or tamari
- 1 tsp vegan Worcestershire sauce
- 2 garlic cloves, minced
- ½ tsp cayenne pepper
- ½ tsp salt
- ½ tsp black pepper
- 1 tsp sugar
- 3 cups florets, cut into bite-sized pieces
- ½ cup peanuts, dry-roasted (for garnish)

In a large pot of salted water, boil the pasta. While pasta is cooking, in a small bowl, whisk together the peanut butter and hot water until smooth. Stir in the Braggs, Worcestershire, garlic, cayenne, salt, pepper, and sugar. Set aside. When pasta is almost done, add the broccoli to the pasta and cook for an additional 3–4 minutes. Drain noodles and broccoli and return to pot. Pour in peanut sauce and toss well. Garnish with chopped peanuts. Makes 2 servings.

Matthew's Spicy Tomato, Peanut & Kale Pasta

I adore this recipe. We have made it for all our friends and it always gets the same response: initial fear and trepidation, and then a rave response as they ask me for the recipe. —Caroline, Eugene, Oregon

- pasta, enough for 2 people
- 1 10-oz (285-mL) can tomato juice, unsweetened
- 2 cups kale, finely chopped
- 2 tbsp peanut butter (or nut butter of choice)
- 1 tsp Asian chili-garlic sauce (or other hot sauce)

In a large pot of salted water, boil the pasta. While pasta is cooking, in a medium pot on medium-high heat, cook the tomato juice and kale for 6–8 minutes or until kale is tender. Stir in the peanut butter and chili sauce until smooth and simmer for an additional 2 minutes. Drain noodles and return to pot. Add the sauce to noodles and toss well. Serve immediately. Makes 2 large or 4 small servings.

Spaghetti & Tofu Balls

I love these! —**Melissa, New York City**

- pasta, enough for 2 people

Tofu balls:
- ½ cup firm tofu, mashed or crumbled
- ¼ cup flour
- ½ tbsp tahini (or nut butter)
- 1 tbsp Braggs or tamari
- ⅛ cup fresh parsley, minced
- 1 very small onion, minced
- ¼ tsp dry mustard
- ⅛ tsp black pepper
- ¼ cup flour (for coating)
- 2 tbsp oil

Pasta sauce:
- 1 small onion, chopped
- 1 tbsp oil
- 1 small carrot, chopped
- 1 celery stalk, chopped
- 2 garlic cloves, chopped
- 1 14-oz (398-mL) can tomato sauce
- ½ tbsp dried basil
- ½ tsp salt
- 1 tsp sweetener (e.g., maple syrup or sugar)
- ¼ cup fresh parsley, minced
- 1 tbsp red wine vinegar

To prepare tofu balls: In a large bowl, stir together the tofu, ¼ cup flour, tahini, Braggs, parsley, onion, mustard, and pepper. Place remaining ¼ cup flour onto a small plate, roll ½ tbsp tofu mixture into a ball, and coat with flour until all tofu mixture is used. In a frying pan on medium heat, fry tofu balls in oil until browned all over. Set aside. In a large pot of salted water, boil the pasta.

To prepare sauce and pasta: While pasta is cooking, in a medium saucepan on medium-high heat, sauté the onion in the oil until translucent. Add the carrot, celery, and garlic, and sauté for an additional 4–6 minutes or until carrot starts to soften. Add the tomato sauce, basil, salt, and sweetener, and simmer over medium-low heat for 15–20 minutes. When ready to serve, turn off heat and stir in the parsley, vinegar, and tofu balls. Let stand 5 minutes before serving over pasta. Makes 2 large or 4 small servings; approx. 8–10 tofu balls.

Roasted Cherry Tomato Pasta
with Kalamata Olives & Capers

A huge winner. I make it all the time.
—Auntie Bonnie, Victoria, British Columbia

- 20–24 cherry tomatoes, halved
- 2 tbsp oil
- 2 garlic cloves, minced
- 2 tsp balsamic vinegar
- ⅛ tsp red pepper flakes
- 1½ tsp dried oregano
- pasta, enough for 2 people
- ¼ cup pitted Kalamata olives, roughly chopped
- 2 tbsp capers, drained
- ¼ cup vegan grated cheese (optional)

Preheat oven to 400°F (205°C). Toss the tomatoes in the oil with garlic, vinegar, red pepper flakes, and oregano and place in an 8x8-in (20x20-cm) pan, cut side up. Bake for 20 minutes. While tomatoes are baking, boil pasta in a large pot of salted water. When pasta is cooked, drain noodles and return to pot. Add the cooked tomatoes, olives, capers, and "cheese" to noodles and toss well. Serve immediately. Makes 2 large or 4 small servings.

Punk-kin Pasta

A lovely alternative to tomato sauce, this tasty pasta will have you wishing you doubled the recipe so you could have leftovers. If you can't find vegan sausage, try throwing in half a small can of beans (your choice) or nothing at all. This sauce is so yum, it can easily stand alone.

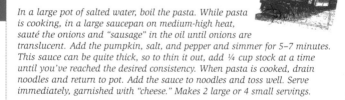

- pasta, enough for 2 people
- 1 medium onion, chopped
- 1 cup vegan sausage, sliced
- 1 tbsp oil
- 1 14-oz (398-mL) can unsweetened pumpkin purée
- ½ tsp salt
- ½ tsp black pepper
- ¼–½ cup vegetable stock (optional)
- ½ cup vegan cheese, grated (optional)

In a large pot of salted water, boil the pasta. While pasta is cooking, in a large saucepan on medium-high heat, sauté the onions and "sausage" in the oil until onions are translucent. Add the pumpkin, salt, and pepper and simmer for 5–7 minutes. This sauce can be quite thick, so to thin it out, add ¼ cup stock at a time until you've reached the desired consistency. When pasta is cooked, drain noodles and return to pot. Add the sauce to noodles and toss well. Serve immediately, garnished with "cheese." Makes 2 large or 4 small servings.

Red Lentil Pasta

Holy time saver, Bat-Girl! This pasta can be made faster then Bruce Wayne gets into his costume, and it is chock full of protein and vitamins. Use whatever noodles you desire.

- noodles, enough for 2 people
- 1 small onion, chopped
- 1 tbsp oil
- 2 garlic cloves, minced
- ¾ cup vegetable stock
- ½ cup dry red lentils
- 1 large tomato, chopped
- ¼ tsp cinnamon
- ¼ tsp salt
- ¼ tsp black pepper
- ½ cup toasted cashews

In a large pot of salted water, boil the noodles. While noodles are cooking, in a medium saucepan on medium heat, sauté the onion in the oil until translucent. Add the garlic, stock, lentils, tomato, cinnamon, salt, and pepper. Bring sauce to a boil, then reduce heat to simmer for 10–12 minutes or until lentils are cooked. With a blender or food processor, blend half or all of the sauce until smooth (be careful when blending hot liquids); return to pot. Reheat and serve over noodles, garnished with cashews. Makes 2 large or 4 small servings.

In a Pinch Avocado Lunch

This isn't a recipe, it's more of a snack tip. I was stuck at a truck stop in California once and the only fresh food they had for sale was avocados. Armed with a plastic knife and a bag of corn chips, I managed to cobble together a nice lunch.

- 1 avocado
- 1 bag of chips or box of crackers

Cut avocado in half and remove pit. Carefully slice avocado flesh vertically and then horizontally, being careful to not pierce the skin. Use chips or crackers to scoop out avocado. Makes 1 serving.

Pita Potato Pizza

The Sullivan Street Bakery in New York City has the most amazing potato pizza on their menu.... I came home from my trip inspired to try to duplicate an über quick and easy version. I use the slicing blade side on my box grater to cut the potato thinly. Proceed with caution, this blade is sharp! Are you down with PPP? Yeah you know me....

- 1 large potato, very thinly sliced
- 1 small onion, thinly sliced
- 3 garlic cloves, minced
- 2 tbsp dried rosemary
- 3 tbsp olive oil
- ½ tsp black pepper
- 4 pitas or 1 pre-baked pizza round
- 1 tsp coarse salt

Preheat oven to 350°F (175°C). Lay out pitas on baking sheet. In a medium bowl stir together the potato, onion, garlic, rosemary, oil, and pepper. Toss well. Layer potato mixture on pitas or pizza round. Top each pita evenly with salt. Bake for 15–25 minutes or until potatoes are cooked. Makes 2 large or 4 small servings.

One Pot Beans & Quinoa

A thrifty and easy recipe that you can make for a quick boost of protein when you're on the road. If you can't find quinoa, then jasmine rice or a quick cooking grain will do. You can also use a different bean if black beans ain't your thang. This recipe is great served on its own or over toast. Good for breakfast, lunch, or dinner.

- 1 small onion, minced
- 2 garlic cloves, minced
- 1 tsp oil
- ⅓ cup vegetable stock or water
- ⅓ cup quinoa
- 1 19-oz (540-mL) can black beans, drained and rinsed
- ½ tsp cumin
- ¼ tsp salt
- ¼ tsp black pepper
- ¼ cup frozen corn
- 1–2 tbsp fresh cilantro, minced

In a medium pot on medium heat, sauté the onions and garlic in the oil until onions are translucent. Add the stock, quinoa, beans, cumin, salt, and pepper. Bring to a boil, then reduce heat and simmer for 15–20 minutes, stirring often to prevent sticking. Remove from heat and stir in corn and cilantro. Makes 1 large or 2 small servings.

Miscellaneous

Entrées

Dragon Bowl

I love this recipe because you can take it camping and most of the veggies can be eaten raw. I bring beets to grate for topping as well and serve it with Shoshana's Spectacular All-Purpose Tahini Sauce (pg 127) or Sarah & Tanya's You-Must-Make-This-Dressing (pg 55).
—Ann, Canton, New York

- 1 cup brown rice
- 2 cups kale, chopped
- 2 medium carrots, grated
- 2 green onion stalks, chopped
- 1 cup firm tofu, cubed
- Dressing or sauce of your choice

Cook rice in a large pot (you'll need the extra space for the veggies). When rice is done, turn off heat and place kale, carrots, onion, and tofu on top of rice. Cover and let sit for 5 minutes. Prepare your dressing or sauce. Assemble each serving bowl with equal parts rice, kale, carrots, onions, and tofu. Top with dressing or sauce. Makes 2 servings

Creamy Curried Veggies

Here's a travel tip! This recipe is easier to make on the road if you snag a couple of soy sauce packets from the food court at the local mall, so you don't have to buy a big bottle of soy sauce. I add a small can of kidney beans to this recipe for extra protein. —Holly, Ottawa, Ontario.

- rice or noodles, enough for 4–6 people
- 1 large onion, sliced
- 2–6 garlic cloves, minced
- 1–3 large carrots, diced
- 2 tbsp oil
- 1 medium potato, cubed
- 1½ cups cauliflower florets, chopped
- 6–8 mushrooms, chopped
- 1 tbsp curry powder
- ½ tsp cumin
- ½ tsp turmeric
- ⅛ tsp cayenne pepper
- 1 14-oz (398-mL) can coconut milk
- 1 cup peas
- 3 tbsp Braggs or tamari

Cook rice or noodles according to package directions. In a large saucepan on medium-high heat, sauté the onions, garlic, and carrots in the oil until onions are translucent. Add the potato, cauliflower, mushrooms, curry, cumin, turmeric, and cayenne, and cook for 2–4 minutes, stirring often to prevent sticking. Add the coconut milk, cover, and reduce heat to medium-low to simmer for 10–20 minutes, stirring occasionally, until potatoes can be pierced easily with a fork. Stir in the peas and Braggs, and cook uncovered on medium-high heat, stirring constantly until the liquid has thickened. Serve over rice or noodles. Makes 4 large or 6 small servings.

Savory Shepherd's Pie

This is my most-used recipe. It's always a crowd pleaser, especially with carnivores, who usually have no idea it's meatless, unless you tell them. So it's great for family dinners and holidays. I offer a miso or mushroom gravy [see pg 128-129] with it when serving to company.
—Erin, Melbourne, Australia

Filling:
- 1 small or medium onion, chopped
- 3 small carrots, chopped
- ½ cup fresh spinach, chopped
- 1 celery stalk, chopped
- 1 large tomato, chopped
- 2 tbsp oil
- ½ cup canned green lentils, drained, rinsed, and mashed
- ½ tsp dried basil
- ½ tsp salt
- 1 tbsp Braggs or tamari

Topping:
- 3 medium potatoes, roughly chopped
- ¼ cup vegan milk
- 1 tbsp vegan margarine or olive oil
- salt (to taste)

Preheat oven to 350°F (175°C). In a medium pot of water, boil the potatoes until they can be pierced easily with a fork. In a medium saucepan, sauté the onion, carrots, spinach, celery, and tomato in the oil. Once carrots are tender, add the mashed lentils, basil, salt, and Braggs. Stir and simmer uncovered until the liquid cooks off. While the vegetables are cooking, mash the potatoes with the "milk," margarine, and salt. Set aside. Pour the vegetable mixture into a lightly oiled pie plate and then layer the mashed potatoes over top. Bake for 15–20 minutes. Makes 4 servings.

Mum's Bean & "Cheese" Casserole

I love Mum's Bean and Cheese Casserole. I first made it six years ago for my husband in our tiny apartment on a freezing day. We warmed our hands on the bowls and opened the oven after cooking to let the heat out to warm the kitchen. It is the perfect tasty, economical meal for a young couple.
—Candyce, Nashville, Tennessee

- 5–6 small potatoes, sliced
- 1 tbsp prepared mustard
- 1 14-oz (398-ml) can baked beans in tomato sauce
- 1 tsp black pepper
- 1–2 cups vegan cheese

Preheat oven to 400°F (205°C). In a large pot of water, boil the sliced potatoes until they can be pierced easily with a fork. Meanwhile, in a small bowl, stir together the mustard, beans, and pepper, and set aside. Drain the potatoes and place half of them in a lightly oiled casserole dish. Layer half of the bean mixture on top, then half of "cheese." Repeat. Cover and bake for 35–40 minutes. Makes 2 large or 4 small servings.

Veggie Pot Pie

My mum and fiancé didn't want me in the kitchen cooking all day on Xmas so I thought this recipe would be good, since I could make it the night before. They ended up eating more of my dish than their non-vegan dish. Too funny, huh? —Taylor, Houston, Texas

Crust:
- 1 cup flour
- ½ tsp salt
- ⅓ cup vegan margarine
- 2 tbsp vegan milk

To prepare crust: In a bowl, combine the flour and salt. Using two knives, cut in the margarine until mixture resembles a coarse meal (you can also do this in a food processor if available). Add "milk" and blend until well combined and dough forms. Remove dough, roll into a ball, and wrap in plastic. Refrigerate for at least 1 hour before using. Preheat oven to 400°F (205°C). Lightly oil a deep dish 10-in (25-cm) pie plate or an 8x8-in (20x20-cm) baking dish and set aside.

Filling:
- 1 small onion, chopped
- 1 tbsp oil
- 2 celery stalks, chopped
- 1 large carrot, chopped
- ½ red bell pepper, chopped
- 1 medium potato, chopped
- ⅓ cup frozen peas
- ¼ cup dry red lentils
- 1 cup vegetable stock
- ½ tsp salt
- ¼ tsp black pepper
- ¼ tsp dried sage
- ¼ tsp dried thyme
- ¼ tsp cayenne pepper
- 2 tbsp flour
- ½ cup vegan milk

To prepare filling: In a large saucepan on medium heat, sauté the onion in the oil until translucent. Add the celery, carrot, and bell pepper and sauté for an additional 2–3 minutes. Add the potato, peas, lentils, stock, salt, pepper, sage, thyme, and cayenne. Bring to a boil, then reduce heat; cover with lid and simmer for 4–6 minutes or until lentils are soft. Stir in the flour and "milk" and simmer until sauce begins to thicken. Transfer filling to baking dish. Roll out dough and place evenly over top of vegetables and bake for 20–25 minutes. Makes 2 large or 4 small servings.

Festive Stuffed Butternut Squash

This recipe takes a little longer, but it's perfect for when you have a little more time to spend on dinner. You can prepare the stuffed squash ahead of time. Serve this festive meal garnished with a scrumptious gravy (pg 128-29).

Miscellaneous

Entrées

- ½ cup brown rice
- 1 small/medium butternut squash
- 1 medium onion, chopped
- 1 garlic clove, minced
- 1 celery stalk, chopped
- ½ small green bell pepper, chopped
- 1 tbsp oil
- ¼ tsp dried basil
- ¼ tsp dried oregano
- ¼ tsp cumin
- 1 tbsp Braggs or tamari
- 3 tsp tahini
- ¼ tsp salt
- ¼ tsp black pepper
- ½ cup walnuts, chopped
- ¼ cup pecans, chopped
- 1 slice of bread, cubed

Preheat oven to 350°F (175°C). In a medium pot, cook the rice. While rice is cooking, wash the outside of the squash thoroughly. Cut the squash in half lengthwise, scoop out the seeds, and place squash cut side down on a lightly oiled baking sheet. Bake in the oven for 20–35 minutes or until squash is tender. Remove squash from the oven (do not turn off oven) and place on cooling rack. Let sit until squash cools down enough to handle, then scoop out flesh (reserve squash shells for later) and place in a large bowl. Set aside. In a large saucepan on medium-high heat, sauté the onions, garlic, celery, and green pepper in the oil until onions are translucent. Add the squash, cooked rice, and remaining ingredients and stir together well. Stuff mixture into hollowed-out squash shells. Return shells to baking sheet and bake for 15–20 minutes. Makes 2 large or 4 small servings.

Tomato Walnut-Crusted Fried "Chicken"

My boyfriend is a total pro at making seitan so we love to make this recipe. It's so simple but delicious! —Caroline, Eugene, Oregon

- 4 Faux Chicken (or Faux Turkey) cutlets (pg 183)
- 3 tbsp oil

Marinade:
- 1 5.5-oz (156-mL) can tomato paste
- 2 tbsp red wine vinegar
- ½ cup juice (e.g., orange or cranberry)
- 2 garlic cloves, minced
- 1 tsp dried rosemary
- 2 tsp No-Salt Shaker (pg 190)

Crust:
- 1 cup walnuts
- ½ cup flour
- 1 tbsp dried rosemary
- ½ tsp salt
- ½ tsp black pepper

In a small bowl, stir together the marinade ingredients. Place "chicken" cutlets on a large plate and pour marinade over top, making sure that both sides are coated well. Marinate for at least 1 hour before cooking. With a blender or food processor, blend the crust ingredients until smooth. Pour into a shallow dish and dip marinated "chicken" into crust, coating both sides. In a large frying pan on medium-high heat, fry "chicken" in the oil until well browned on both sides. Makes 2 large or 4 small servings.

Classic Spinach Lasagna

*This is so easy to make and tastes soooo good. I've given the recipe to my
mother-in-law, a recently converted vegetarian, who makes it for family
gatherings and it's always a big hit!* —Dominique via MySpace

- 1 lb (455 g) firm tofu
- ¼ cup vegan milk
- 1 tsp dried oregano
- 3 tsp dried basil
- 1 tsp salt
- 2 tbsp lemon juice
- 4 garlic cloves, minced
- 1 small onion, chopped
- 2 cups fresh spinach, chopped
- 4–6 cups tomato sauce
- cooked lasagna noodles
- 2 cups vegan cheese, grated (optional)

*Preheat oven to 350°F (175°C). With a blender or food processor, blend the
tofu, "milk," oregano, basil, salt, lemon juice, garlic, and onion together
until mixture achieves the consistency of cottage cheese. If the mixture is too
thick, add a little water. Stir in the spinach and set aside. Cover the bottom
of a lasagna pan with a thin layer of tomato sauce, then place a layer of
noodles on top. Sprinkle with half the tofu mixture and ½ cup "cheese." Cover
this with another layer of noodles, then sauce. Sprinkle with the remaining
tofu mixture, another ½ cup "cheese," and another layer of sauce. Add one
more layer of noodles, and cover with remaining sauce. Top with remaining
"cheese." Bake for 30–45 minutes. Remove from oven and let sit for 10
minutes before serving. Makes 4–6 servings.*

Wendy's Lentil & Brown Rice Casserole

I make this all the time as I always have these ingredients stockpiled in my cupboards. We have it either as a side dish or as a meal on its own. My entire family loves it. —**Sheila, Lake Country, British Columbia**

- ¾ cup dry red lentils
- ¾ cup brown rice
- 1 medium onion, chopped
- 3 cups vegetable stock
- 1 14-oz (398-mL) can crushed tomatoes
- ½ tsp dried basil
- ½ tsp dried oregano
- ¾ cup vegan cheese, grated (optional)

Preheat oven to 350°F (175°C). In a large casserole dish, combine the lentils, rice, onion, stock, tomatoes, basil, oregano, and stir to combine. Cover with lid and bake for 1½ hours (stirring every half-hour). Remove lid, sprinkle with "cheese," and broil uncovered until "cheese" has melted. (Keep an eye on it so it doesn't burn.) Makes 2 large or 4 small servings.

Sarah's Delicious Chili

Sooo easy to make this away from home. All you need is canned foods and a few fresh veggies. I made this recipe at my omni parents' house over Christmas and the only ingredient they didn't have was curry paste. It was a hit!
—**Holly, Ottawa, Ontario**

- 1 medium onion, chopped
- 2 medium carrots, chopped
- 1 tbsp oil
- 2 19-oz (540-mL) cans beans (e.g., kidney or black), drained and rinsed
- 1 28-oz (796-mL) can diced tomatoes
- 1 5.5-oz (156-mL) can tomato paste
- 1 19-oz (540-mL) can chickpeas (garbanzo beans), drained and rinsed
- 8–12 mushrooms, chopped
- 1 12-oz (340-mL) can corn
- ¾ cup rice
- 1–3 tbsp chili powder
- 1 tbsp black pepper
- 2 tbsp curry paste
- 2 cups vegetable stock or water

In a large pot on medium-high heat, sauté the onions and carrots in oil until onions are translucent. Add the remaining ingredients and stir together. Reduce heat to medium-low and simmer for 40–60 minutes, stirring occasionally. Makes 6–8 servings.

Tip-Top Tofu Loaf

Is there any other word in the English language that is less appetizing than "loaf"? Despite the name, this easy and delish dish can be thrown together and on your table to eat in about an hour. It also makes a great sandwich filler (pg 89).

- 2 tbsp oil
- 1 cup medium-firm tofu, drained
- 1 small onion, roughly chopped
- 2 garlic cloves, roughly chopped
- 2 tbsp ketchup
- 2 tbsp Braggs or tamari
- 1 tbsp Dijon mustard
- ¼ cup fresh parsley, chopped
- ¼ tsp black pepper
- ½ cup rolled oat flakes or bread crumbs
- 1 tbsp tahini

Preheat oven to 350°F (175°C). Oil a 9-in (23 cm) loaf pan with the oil (leaving excess in the pan) and set aside. In a food processor, blend together the remaining ingredients until well mixed. Pour into baking dish, pressing mixture down evenly. Bake for 55–60 minutes. Let cool 10 minutes before serving. Makes approx. 2 large or 4 small servings.

Miscellaneous

Entrées

Tofu Roast

This recipe is amazing. Even my omnivore father says it's the best thing I've ever made. —Lauren, Farmington Valley, Connecticut

- 2 lb (910 g) firm or extra firm tofu
- 2 tbsp Braggs or tamari
- 1 tsp dried sage

Stuffing:
- 1 small onion, minced
- 4 large button mushrooms, chopped
- 1 small carrot, diced
- 1 celery stalk, minced
- 1½ tbsp oil
- ½ cup golden raisins
- 2 garlic cloves, minced
- 2 tbsp Braggs or tamari
- 1 tsp dried sage
- 1 tsp dried rosemary
- ½ tsp dried thyme
- 3 cups bread, cubed
- ¼ cup walnuts, roughly chopped
- 1 cup vegetable stock

Basting sauce:
- ¼ cup dark sesame oil
- ¼ cup olive oil
- ¼ cup Braggs or tamari
- 1 tbsp miso
- 2 tbsp cranberry or orange juice
- 1 tsp Dijon mustard
- ½ tsp liquid smoke (optional)
- ¼ tsp black pepper

Carefully squeeze the tofu to remove as much water as possible. Line a large colander with a dampened cheesecloth so that the cheesecloth hangs over the sides. Place colander on a large plate. Roughly chop tofu, place inside colander, and cover with cheesecloth. Place something heavy (e.g., 2 unopened soy milk boxes) on top to press any remaining liquid out of tofu. Let sit for an hour.

To prepare stuffing and assemble roast: In a large saucepan on medium heat, sauté the onions, mushrooms, carrot, and celery in the oil until onions are translucent. Add the remaining ingredients and reduce heat to simmer for 5–6 minutes or until liquid has been absorbed. Set aside. With a food processor, blend the drained tofu, Braggs, and sage until smooth. Remove ½ cup of the tofu mixture and set aside for later. Return the remaining blended tofu to the cheesecloth-covered colander and press it down against the edges of the colander—leaving a 1-in (2½-cm) thick shell, creating a bowl shape. Add the cooked stuffing to the center of the tofu bowl and press reserved ½ cup tofu over top to cover stuffing. Smooth tofu over so stuffing is sealed inside. Carefully bring up the edges of the cheesecloth, tying it VERY tightly, and place colander on a large plate. Place a smaller plate on top of roast and put weight back on top of the cheesecloth in order to press out any remaining liquid, and refrigerate for at least 3 hours (overnight is better).

To prepare sauce and bake roast: Preheat oven to 450°F (230°C). In a small bowl, whisk together the basting sauce ingredients. Set aside. Line a baking pan with tin foil. Remove roast from fridge and carefully remove from cheesecloth. Place roast flat side down on pan and baste with half the sauce. Cover with foil and bake for 1 hour. Reduce heat to 350°F (175°C). Remove foil and baste with remaining sauce. Bake for an additional 30 minutes, basting every 10 minutes with run-off sauce. Carefully transfer roast to a serving platter. Makes 6–8 servings.

Jay-Lo's Fried "Chicken"

This is my friend Jason's recipe, which he makes for BBQs on his "vegans only" grill. It's delish and quite a dish … just like Jay.

- ¼ cup flour
- ½ tsp paprika
- ½ tsp salt
- ½ tsp black pepper
- ½ cup vegan milk
- Faux Chicken cutlets (pg 183)
- 3–4 tbsp oil

In a shallow dish, combine the flour, paprika, salt, and pepper and set aside. In a small bowl, pour "milk" and set aside. Dip "chicken" into flour, then dip in "milk," and then into flour again. In a large frying pan on medium-high heat, fry coated "chicken" in the oil until well browned on both sides. Makes 2 large or 4 small servings.

Stuffed Cabbage Rolls

My sister who doesn't eat much of anything but cookies and ice cream loves this recipe. I think that's a good sign. Ha!
—**Lauren, Farmington Valley, Connecticut**

- 1 small head of green cabbage

Filling:
- ¼ cup bulgur
- ¼ cup boiling water
- 1 small onion
- 2 garlic cloves, minced
- 3 large button mushrooms, minced
- 1 tbsp oil
- 1 tbsp Braggs or tamari
- ⅛ tsp paprika
- ⅛ tsp black pepper
- ⅛ tsp cayenne pepper
- 3 tbsp walnuts, finely chopped
- ½ cup cooked cabbage, finely chopped

Sauce:
- 2 large garlic cloves, minced
- 2 tbsp olive oil
- 1 14-oz (398-mL) can diced tomatoes
- 1 5.5-oz (156-mL) can tomato paste
- 1 tsp sweetener (e.g., maple syrup or sugar)
- ¼ tsp salt
- ¼ tsp black pepper

Preheat oven to 350°F (175°C). Remove core from the cabbage and steam whole head for 20 minutes. Set aside to cool. Remove 6 large outer leaves and set aside.

To prepare the filling: In a small bowl, pour boiling water over bulgur. Cover with lid and set aside. In a medium saucepan on medium heat, sauté the onions, garlic, and mushrooms in the oil until onions are translucent. Add the Braggs, paprika, pepper, cayenne, walnuts, and bulgur and sauté for 6–8 minutes. Add ½ cup of the cooked minced cabbage and set aside.

To prepare the sauce: In a medium saucepan on medium-low heat, sauté the garlic in the oil until translucent. Add the remaining ingredients and bring to a boil. Reduce heat to low and simmer for 15–20 minutes.

Assemble cabbage rolls by dividing filling among the 6 reserved leaves. Roll each leaf and arrange in a lightly oiled 8x8-in (20-cm) baking dish. Spoon sauce evenly over top and bake for 20–25 minutes. Makes 2 large or 4 small servings; sauce makes approx. 2 cups.

Portobello Mushroom Bake

I don't even have words to tell you how good this recipe is, well, except maybe "yowza"! —Erin, Vancouver, British Columbia

- ½ cup almonds
- ¼ cup oil
- ¼ cup Braggs or tamari
- ¼–½ cup water
- 2 tbsp balsamic vinegar
- 3 garlic cloves, roughly chopped
- 1 tsp dried rosemary
- 1 tsp dried oregano
- 4 large Portobello mushrooms, stems removed
- 1 medium onion, sliced

Preheat oven to 350°F (175°C). With a blender or food processor, blend the almonds until powdered. Add the oil, Braggs, water, vinegar, garlic, rosemary, and oregano, and blend until well combined. In a large baking dish, place the mushrooms upside down and top with onion. Pour sauce over top and bake for 20–25 minutes. Makes 2 large or 4 small servings.

Tanya's Asian Creation

When Tanya was in Japan she had a difficult time finding food, but thank goodness she did because she came up with this simple and delish recipe while strolling through the markets looking for food she could eat. This is one of my favorites from *HIAV*.

- buckwheat noodles, enough for 4 people
- 2 cups cubed squash
  (e.g., kuri, kabocha, butternut, or acorn; don't use spaghetti squash)
- 2 tbsp oil (for sautéing)
- 1 lb (455 g) firm tofu, cubed
- 1–3 tsp black pepper
- 1 tsp salt
- 3 green onion stalks, chopped
- 4 tbsp oil (e.g., flax or hemp)
- Braggs or tamari (for garnish)
- gomashio (for garnish) (pg 189)

In a medium pot on high heat, boil the noodles according to package directions. Meanwhile, in a medium saucepan on high heat, sauté the squash in the oil for about 5 minutes, then add the tofu, pepper, and salt. Continue cooking until squash can be easily pierced with a fork. Add the onions, cover with lid, and set aside. When noodles are ready, rinse in hot water, then return to pot and toss with the oil to prevent noodles from sticking. Transfer noodles to a bowl or plate and top with squash mixture, then garnish with Braggs and gomashio. Makes 2 large or 4 small servings.

Sauces

DRESS ACCORDINGLY

Sun-Dried Tomato Pesto

I love making pasta salad with this pesto.
—Melissa, New York City

- 2 cups fresh basil
- 6–8 sun-dried tomatoes, rehydrated
- 3 garlic cloves
- ¼ tsp salt
- ¼ cup olive oil
- ¼ cup pine nuts, toasted

With a blender or food processor, blend the basil, tomatoes, garlic, salt, oil, and ½ of the pine nuts until coarsely mixed. Stir in remaining pine nuts. Makes approx. 1 cup.

Tyler & Phoebe's Perfect Pesto Sauce

A simple, quick, versatile sauce that can be tossed with noodles or potato salad, or used as a sandwich spread or as an alternative to tomato sauce on pizza. My favorite way to use this sauce is on Nana's Pesto Pinwheel Rolls (pg 139).

- 3 cups fresh basil
- ¼–½ cup pine nuts, toasted
- 2–4 garlic cloves
- ½ tsp salt
- ½ tsp black pepper
- ½ cup olive oil

With a blender or food processor, blend all ingredients, drizzling in oil gradually, until well mixed. Makes approx. 1 cup.

Fresh Five-Minute Basil Tomato Sauce

This simple, fresh, no-cook sauce can be whizzed together in a matter of minutes. To add a little weight to this sauce, I'll sometimes throw in some tofu.

- 4 medium tomatoes
- 2 tbsp olive oil
- 2 garlic cloves
- ¼ cup fresh basil (tightly packed)
- ½ tsp salt
- ½ tsp black pepper

Chop one of the tomatoes and set aside for later. With a blender or food processor, blend together the remaining tomatoes, oil, garlic, basil, salt, and pepper until chunky. Add the sauce and the reserved chopped tomato, and toss well. Serve immediately. Makes approx. 2 cups.

Ginger Peanut Sauce

This sure hit, containing a lovely combination of flavors, can be used for stir-fries, noodles, or anything you can think of.

* 1 small onion, chopped
* 2 garlic cloves, minced
* ½ tbsp oil
* ½ cup hot water
* ¼ tsp curry powder
* ½ tbsp fresh ginger, grated
* ½ cup peanut butter (or other nut butter)
* 1½ tbsp Braggs or tamari
* ½ tbsp sesame oil
* ⅛ tsp cayenne pepper

In a medium saucepan on medium heat, sauté the onions and garlic in the oil until onions are translucent. Stir in the remaining ingredients and whisk or stir until smooth. Simmer for 5 minutes on medium heat, stirring often to prevent sticking. Makes approx. 1 cup.

Claire's Cheeze Sauce

Yum. Yum. Yum.

- 3 tbsp vegan margarine
- 3 tbsp flour
- ½ tsp salt
- ¼ tsp black pepper
- 1½ cups vegan milk
- 1 cup vegan cheese, grated
- ½ tsp Dijon mustard (optional)

In a small saucepan on medium heat, melt the margarine. Once margarine is liquefied, remove from heat (don't turn the burner off) and add the flour, salt, and pepper; whisk until smooth. Return saucepan to burner and slowly add ½ cup of "milk," whisking constantly until thickening occurs, then add remaining "milk," ½ cup at a time. Cook sauce over medium heat, whisking constantly until thickened and smooth. Add the "cheese" and mustard and cook for an additional 5 minutes, whisking until smooth and well blended. Makes approx. 2 cups.

Wolffie's Nutritional-Yeast "Cheese" Sauce

A versatile, cheesy sauce to serve over burritos, pasta, burgers, or veggies—actually, anything you can think of.

- ½ cup nutritional yeast flakes
- 2 tbsp flour
- ½ tsp salt
- 1 cup water
- 2 tsp oil
- 1½ tsp Dijon mustard
- 1½ tsp Braggs or tamari

In a small saucepan on high heat, whisk together all ingredients. Bring to a boil, then reduce heat to simmer for 2–4 minutes, stirring constantly. Makes approx. 1½ cups.

Shoshana's Spectacular All-Purpose Tahini Sauce

Here's a wonderful sauce I pour over lentils, quinoa, or steamed veggies. It's awesome! —Shoshana, *themonkeybunch.com*

- ½ cup shallots (or 1 small onion), roughly chopped
- 2 garlic cloves, roughly chopped
- 1 tbsp dark sesame oil
- ¼ cup lemon juice
- 3 tbsp Braggs or tamari
- ⅓ cup tahini
- 1 tbsp maple syrup
- ¼ cup vegetable stock
- ¼ cup olive oil
- ¼ cup oil (e.g., flax or hemp)

In a small saucepan on medium heat, sauté the shallots and garlic in the oil until shallots are translucent. With a blender or food processor, blend the shallots and remaining ingredients until smooth and creamy. Makes approx. 1½ cups.

Mighty Miso Gravy

This is a holiday staple for us. Even my very meat-eating in-laws are so impressed with this one that it's become an expected part of our holiday dinners. —Sheila, Lake Country, British Columbia

- 6–10 mushrooms, finely chopped
- 1 medium onion, finely chopped
- 1 tbsp oil
- 2–3 tbsp Braggs or tamari
- ¼ tsp dried basil
- ¼ tsp dried dill
- ¼ tsp cayenne pepper
- ¼ tsp black pepper
- ⅓–½ cup flour
- 1⅓ cups vegetable stock or water
- 1 tsp miso

In a medium saucepan on medium-high heat, sauté the mushrooms and onions in the oil until onions are translucent and mushrooms are tender. Add the Braggs, basil, dill, cayenne, and pepper and stir to combine. Remove from heat and slowly stir in the flour, mixing well until it becomes pasty and dry. Slowly stir in the stock a little at a time until well mixed with no lumps. Return saucepan to medium heat and simmer until sauce is thickened, stirring often. At the last minute, stir in miso and serve. Makes 2 cups.

Sauces

Malloreigh's Mushroom Gravy

One of my favorite recipes to make for my family when I visit. They think vegans don't eat yummy food and this recipe shuts them up.
—Candice, Duncan, British Columbia

- 4–6 button mushrooms, finely chopped
- 2 tbsp vegan margarine
- 3 tbsp flour
- 1 tbsp nutritional yeast
- ¼ tsp black pepper
- 1 tsp Braggs or tamari
- 1 cup vegetable stock

In a medium saucepan on medium-high heat, sauté the mushrooms in margarine until soft. Add the flour, nutritional yeast, pepper, and Braggs, and stir constantly until thickened. Whisk in stock ¼ cup at a time, stirring constantly until thickened. Transfer to a blender or food processor to blend if you want smooth gravy, or serve as is. Makes approx. 1½ cups.

Sauces

Barbecue Sauce

*I tried the Barbecue Tofu and, oh my gosh, how awesome! And I loooooove
this sauce recipe.* —Taylor, Houston, Texas

- ¼ cup apple cider vinegar
- 3 tbsp tomato paste
- 3 tbsp maple syrup
- 2 tbsp molasses
- 1 tbsp Braggs or tamari
- 1 tbsp Dijon mustard
- ½ tsp garlic powder
- ½ tsp liquid smoke
- ½ tsp vegan Worcestershire sauce

*In a small saucepan on high heat, combine all the ingredients and bring to
a boil while continuously whisking. Reduce heat to medium-low and simmer
until desired thickness is achieved. Makes approx. ¾ cup.*

DON'T FORGET YOUR MAD MONEY

Nutty Broccoli

I scarf down this dish whenever I make it, so I have to limit the number of times I make it. —Melissa, New York City

- 2 tbsp peanut butter (or other nut butter)
- 1 tbsp Braggs or tamari
- 1 tbsp orange or apple juice
- 4 cups broccoli, chopped

In a small saucepan on medium heat, stir together the nut butter, Braggs, and juice. Heat until warmed through. Meanwhile, steam broccoli for about 3 minutes until it is tender but not fragile. Drain broccoli and toss with sauce. Makes 1 large or 2 small servings.

Larry's Refried Beans

Our friend Larry thinks he knows everything. Well, he sure knows his beans. Serve over rice or in burritos.

- 1 19-oz (540-mL) can beans (e.g., pinto or black), drained and rinsed
- ½ cup vegetable stock or water
- 2 garlic cloves, minced
- ½ cup fresh cilantro, chopped
- 1 tsp cumin
- ¼ tsp cayenne pepper
- 1 Roma tomato, sliced

In a medium pot on medium heat, combine all the ingredients and cook for 10–15 minutes, stirring occasionally. Remove from heat. Mash with a fork, and serve. Makes 2 large or 4 small servings.

Side Dishes

Maury's Roasted Root Vegetables

I love, love, love this one because it not only tastes amazing but it makes the whole house smell yummy while it cooks.
—Erin, Vancouver, British Columbia

- 1 large yam, cubed
- 1 cup parsnips, cubed
- 3 new potatoes, cubed (approx. 1 cup)
- 1 small onion, chopped
- 3 garlic cloves, minced
- 2 tsp dried rosemary
- ½ tsp salt
- ½ tsp black pepper
- 2 tbsp grapeseed or olive oil

Preheat oven to 400°F (205°C). In a medium baking dish, toss together all the ingredients until veggies are well coated. Bake in oven for 25–30 minutes or until veggies can be pierced easily with a fork. Makes 2 large or 4 small servings.

Mushroom Pâté

Almost all of these ingredients can be found at a conventional grocery store, and it can be served with sliced pita, crackers, or bread. It also makes a great sandwich filler (pg 89).

- 1 cup vegetable stock
- 1 red onion, chopped
- 2 garlic cloves, roughly chopped
- 1 cup button mushrooms, roughly chopped
- 1 cup shiitake mushrooms, roughly chopped
- 1 tsp dried sage
- 1 tsp dried rosemary
- 1 tsp nutmeg
- ½ tsp ground thyme
- 1 tsp salt
- ½ tsp black pepper
- 1 cup walnuts, toasted
- 1 tbsp Braggs or tamari
- 2 tsp balsamic vinegar
- 1 tbsp ground flax seeds
- 1 slice of bread, roughly chopped

In a large saucepan on medium-high heat, bring the stock to a boil. Add the onion, garlic, mushrooms, sage, rosemary, nutmeg, thyme, salt, and pepper and simmer for 8–10 minutes or until liquid has been absorbed and has evaporated. In a food processor, blend mushroom mixture, walnuts, Braggs, vinegar, flax seeds, and bread until smooth. Press evenly into an 8-in (20-cm) loaf pan (or a fancy serving dish with a 2-in [5-cm] lip) and refrigerate for at least 2 hours before serving. Makes 1 loaf.

Cumin Fried Potatoes

A perfect dish to serve alongside Tip-Top Tofu Loaf (pg 115).

- 1 ½ tsp cumin seeds
- 1 tbsp oil
- 1 small onion, chopped
- 1 large potato, cubed
- ½ cup frozen peas
- ¼ tsp salt

In a large saucepan on medium-high heat, dry roast the cumin seeds until they start to pop and brown, watching carefully so they don't burn. Carefully add the oil, onions, and potatoes to saucepan. Cover with lid and sauté, stirring occasionally to avoid sticking, until potatoes are browned and can be pierced easily with a fork. Turn off heat, add the peas and salt, and cover with lid. Let sit 5 minutes before serving. Makes 1 large or 2 small servings.

Barbecue Tofu

I like to freeze a block of tofu before I make this recipe to change the texture. It is wonderful—I used my grill pan to grill up the tofu and it was amazing! Okay, I will stop now … hahaha! —Taylor, Houston, Texas

- 1 lb (455 g) firm tofu, cubed or sliced
- ½ cup barbecue sauce (pg 130)
- 1 tbsp oil

In a small bowl, combine the tofu and sauce and stir until tofu is well coated. Marinate for 5 minutes. In a medium saucepan on medium-high heat, sauté the tofu and sauce in the oil until the tofu is browned. Makes 2 large or 4 small servings.

Caramelized Onion & Fennel Mashed Potatoes

This is my all-time fav way to serve mashed potatoes to my carnivorous family. They fall off their seats when they eat this!
—**Sally, Las Vegas, Nevada**

- 3–4 medium potatoes, cubed
- 1 medium onion, chopped
- 1 small fennel bulb, finely chopped
- 1 tsp sugar
- 1 tsp salt
- ½ tsp black pepper
- 2 tbsp oil
- ½ cup vegan milk
- 2 tbsp oil (e.g. flax or hemp)

In a large pot of water on high heat, boil the potatoes until they can be pierced easily with a fork. Meanwhile, in a large saucepan on medium heat, sauté the onions, fennel, sugar, salt, and pepper in oil until onions are translucent. Set aside. When potatoes are ready, drain them and return to pot. Add "milk" and oil to potatoes and mash. Stir in onion mixture and mix well. Makes 2 large or 4 small servings.

Mashed Garlic Potatoes with Kale

This recipe has been part of my cooking repertoire for so long I forgot that it came from HIAV! —Siue, dairyfreedesserts.com

- 2 medium potatoes, roughly chopped
- 1 small onion, chopped
- 2 garlic cloves, minced
- 1 tbsp oil
- 1 cup kale (about 2–3 stalks), finely chopped
- ¼ cup vegan milk
- 1 tbsp oil (e.g., flax or hemp) or vegan margarine
- 1 tbsp Braggs or tamari
- salt (to taste)
- black pepper (to taste)

In a large pot of water on high heat, boil the potatoes until they can be pierced easily with a fork. Meanwhile, in a medium saucepan on medium heat, sauté the onions and garlic in the oil until onions are translucent. Add the kale and cover with lid. Reduce heat to simmer for 5–10 minutes until kale becomes soft. Set aside. When potatoes are ready, drain and place them in a large bowl. Add "milk," oil, Braggs, salt, and pepper to potatoes and mash. Stir in the kale mixture and mix well. Makes 2 large or 4 small servings.

Side Dishes

Baking & Desserts

WEAR CLEAN UNDERWEAR

Nana's Pesto Pinwheel Rolls

A great recipe for impressing your family with your baking skills. These taste like you went to culinary school, but can be made in mere minutes!

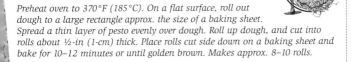

- vegan puff pastry dough, thawed
- ½ cup pesto (pg 122)

Preheat oven to 370°F (185°C). On a flat surface, roll out dough to a large rectangle approx. the size of a baking sheet. Spread a thin layer of pesto evenly over dough. Roll up dough, and cut into rolls about ½-in (1-cm) thick. Place rolls cut side down on a baking sheet and bake for 10–12 minutes or until golden brown. Makes approx. 8–10 rolls.

Kissing Cousins Oat Bread

Oats are a distant cousin of the wheat family, but that doesn't stop them from marrying each other in this easy-to-make loaf.

- 2 cups rolled oat flakes
- 2 cups flour
- 1 tbsp baking powder
- 1 tsp salt
- 3 tbsp maple syrup
- 2 tbsp oil
- 2 cups vegan milk

Preheat oven to 450°F (230°C). Lightly oil a 9-in (23-cm) loaf pan and set aside. In a food processor, grind the oat flakes until smooth and set aside. In a medium bowl, stir together the oat flakes, flour, baking powder, and salt. Add the syrup, oil, and "milk" and gently stir dough until just mixed. Pour evenly into loaf pan and bake for 25–30 minutes or until a toothpick or knife inserted in center comes out clean. Makes 1 loaf.

Easy Biscuits

You must include your Easy Biscuits from HIAV. They use ingredients everyone has on hand. My family asks for them every Saturday. We serve them "Southern style" with gravy or even plain with a smear of jam.
—Annie, Garrett, Indiana

- 2 cups flour
- 3 tsp baking powder
- 1 tsp salt
- ¼ cup vegan margarine or vegetable shortening
- ¾–1 cup sour "milk" (vegan milk + 1 tsp vinegar)

Preheat oven to 450°F (230°C). In a large bowl, sift together the flour, baking powder, and salt. Add the margarine and sour "milk" and mix together gently until just mixed. Spoon into lightly oiled muffin pans, or roll out on a cutting board, cut with biscuit or cookie cutters, and place on a lightly oiled cookie sheet. Bake for 12–18 minutes. Makes 6 biscuits.

Miki's Pumpkin Bread

Another great one that I took to work and was scarfed down in about four seconds by my coworkers. —Melissa, New York City

- 2 cups sugar
- ½ cup oil
- ½ cup applesauce
- egg replacer to equal 3 eggs (pg 177)
- 1 14-oz (398-mL) can unsweetened pumpkin purée
- 3 cups flour
- 1 tsp ground cloves
- 1 tsp cinnamon
- 1 tsp nutmeg
- 1 tsp baking soda
- ½ tsp baking powder
- ½ tsp salt
- 1 cup walnuts, roughly chopped
- 1 cup vegan chocolate chips (optional)

Preheat oven to 350°F (175°C). Lightly oil two 9-in (23-cm) loaf pans and set aside. In a large bowl, stir together the sugar, oil, applesauce, egg replacer, and pumpkin. In a medium bowl, stir together the flour, cloves, cinnamon, nutmeg, baking soda and powder, and salt. Gently stir dry mixture into wet until just mixed. Stir in the walnuts and chocolate chips and spoon dough equally into 2 prepared loaf pans. Bake for 55–60 minutes or until a toothpick or knife inserted in each center comes out clean. Let cool for 10–15 minutes before removing from pan. Makes 2 loaves.

Maureen's Coffee Cake

This dish has become a favorite for me to make on Christmas for my family.
—Melissa, New York City

- ⅓ cup soft tofu
- 1 cup vegan milk
- 1 tbsp apple cider vinegar
- 2½ cups flour
- 1¼ cups sugar
- 3 tsp cinnamon
- 1½ tsp ground ginger
- ½ tsp salt
- ¾ cup oil
- ¾ cup walnuts, chopped
- 1 tsp baking powder
- 1 tsp baking soda

Preheat oven to 350°F (175°C). With a blender or food processor, blend the tofu, "milk," and vinegar until smooth. Set aside. In a large bowl, stir together the flour, sugar, cinnamon, ginger, salt, and oil. Take 1 cup of this mixture and place in a medium bowl, and stir in walnuts and set aside. Add the baking soda and powder to the remaining non-walnut mixture, then add the tofu mixture and mix well. Spread this in a lightly oiled 9x13-in (23x33-cm) baking dish and sprinkle with the reserved walnut mixture. Bake for 30–40 minutes. Makes 1 cake or enough for 1 husband.

Banana Bread

I make this recipe so often that I feel like I wrote the recipe. Ha! Whenever friends are over for coffee they always request it and are amazed that it's vegan. —Lisa, Guelph, Ontario

- 3 ripe bananas
- 1 tbsp lemon juice
- ½ cup oil
- ½ cup sugar
- ¾ cup dates, chopped
- 1½ cups flour
- ½ cup wheat germ
- ½ tsp salt
- ½ tsp baking powder
- ½ tsp baking soda

Preheat oven to 375°F (190°C). In a small bowl, stir together the mashed banana, lemon juice, oil, sugar, and dates. In a separate large bowl, stir together the flour, wheat germ, salt, and baking powder and soda. Add the banana mixture to the flour mixture and stir gently until just mixed. Spoon into a lightly oiled 9-in (23-cm) loaf pan and bake for 40–50 minutes until a toothpick or knife inserted in center comes out clean. Makes 1 loaf.

Delightful Banana Nut Muffins

Everyone I know makes these because I've shared the recipe so much!
—Sarah, *livelightlytour.com*

- 1⅓ cups flour
- ½ cup sugar
- 1 tsp baking powder
- 1 tsp baking soda
- ½ tsp salt
- ¾ cup oat bran
- ½ cup walnuts, chopped
- 2 bananas, mashed well
- ⅓ cup oil
- 1 tsp vanilla extract
- ⅔ cup vegan milk

Preheat oven to 375°F (190°C). In a large bowl, stir together the flour, sugar, baking powder and soda, salt, bran, and walnuts. Add the mashed bananas, oil, vanilla, and "milk," and mix gently until just mixed. Spoon into a lightly oiled muffin pan and bake for 15–20 minutes. Makes 12 muffins.

"Anything Goes" Fruit-Filled Muffins

I adore these muffins. I normally make them first thing Monday morning so the kids and I have healthy snacks to start off our week. Just check out my blog to see how often I mention them. —mamasvillage.blogspot.com

Note: Here are some suggestions for fruit combinations for your muffins: apple-raisin, banana-chocolate chip, raspberry-blackberry, strawberry-apricot, pear-apple, and ginger-apple-apricot.

• 2 cups flour
• ½ tsp salt
• 3 tsp baking powder
• ½ cup sugar
• egg replacer to equal 2 eggs (pg 177)
• ¼ cup oil
• ¾ cup sour "milk" (vegan milk + 1 tsp vinegar)
• 1½ cups fresh or frozen fruit of your choice

Preheat oven to 350°F (175°C). In a large bowl, stir together the flour, salt, and baking powder. Add the sugar, egg replacer, oil, sour "milk," and fruit. Stir until just mixed. Scoop into a lightly oiled muffin pan and bake for 35–45 minutes until a toothpick or fork inserted in center comes out clean. Makes 6 muffins.

Classic Chocolate Chip Cookies

We love this recipe. Whenever we have company coming over they always request these cookies and most guests leave with a few stashed in their pockets. —Steve, Phoenix, Arizona

- ¾ cup sugar
- ½ cup vegan margarine
- ½ cup oil
- 3 tbsp water
- 2 tsp vanilla extract
- 2¼ cups flour
- 1 tsp baking soda
- ½ tsp salt
- 1–1½ cups vegan chocolate chips

Preheat oven to 375°F (190°C). In a small bowl, stir together the sugar, margarine, oil, water, and vanilla. In a large bowl, mix together the flour, baking soda, and salt. Add the margarine mixture and chocolate chips and mix well. Scoop spoon-sized portions onto an unoiled cookie sheet and bake for 8–10 minutes or until the edges are browned. Let cookies cool before removing from sheet. Makes 6 large or 12 small cookies.

Ginger Snaps

This is the one recipe I always make for friends and family over the holidays. Not that your recipe isn't perfect, but I usually add a tiny pinch of cinnamon, nutmeg, cloves, and cardamom too. One time I even replaced the maple syrup with agave nectar for a guest who was diabetic, and they were delicious! —**Laura, Calgary, Alberta (by way of Montreal)**

- 2½ cups flour
- 1 tsp baking powder
- 1 tsp baking soda
- ½ tsp salt
- ¾ cup maple syrup
- ¼ cup molasses
- ½ cup oil
- ⅓ cup fresh ginger, finely grated

Preheat oven to 350°F (175°C). In a large bowl, stir together the flour, baking powder and soda, and salt. Add the syrup, molasses, oil, and ginger. Stir gently until just mixed. Scoop spoon-sized portions onto a lightly oiled cookie sheet and bake for 12–15 minutes. Makes 6 large or 12 small cookies.

Mama Mayhem's Perfectly Easy No-Bake Cookies

A super easy dessert with conventional ingredients that everyone has in their cupboards. —Holly, Ottawa, Ontario

- ½ cup sugar
- ½ tsp vanilla
- ¼ cup vegan milk
- ¼ cup nut butter (your choice)
- ¼ cup vegan margarine
- 2 tsp unsweetened cocoa powder
- 1½ cups quick oats
- 1 cup walnuts, finely chopped

Place a sheet of parchment or wax paper on a cookie sheet and set aside. In a medium saucepan on medium-low heat, melt the sugar, vanilla, "milk," nut butter, margarine, and cocoa powder. Once melted, remove from heat, add the oats and walnuts, and stir until well blended. Drop rounded tablespoonfuls of dough onto prepared cookie sheet and press down flat with your fingers; repeat process until all dough is used. Refrigerate for at least 1 hour before serving. Makes 8 large cookies.

Maureen's Oatmeal Chocolate Chip Cookies

Yesterday I made these cookies for a friend's party. The omnivores were flipping out at how amazing the cookies tasted (of course) then I revealed that myself and the cookies are vegan! Their jaws literally dropped (I love that) as they proceeded to say that they had no idea that cookies could be this good without milk, eggs, and butter. —Melissa, New York City

- ¾ cup flour
- ½ cup sugar
- 2 cups rolled oat flakes
- ½ tsp baking soda
- ½ tsp baking powder
- ½ tsp salt
- ⅓ cup soft tofu or ½ banana
- ⅓ cup oil
- ½ cup maple syrup
- 1 tbsp vanilla extract
- 1–1½ cups vegan chocolate chips (or carob chips)

Preheat oven to 350°F (175°C). In a large bowl, stir together the flour, sugar, rolled oats, baking soda and powder, and salt. With a food processor, blend the tofu, oil, syrup, and vanilla. Pour wet mixture into dry and stir to combine. Add the chocolate chips and stir until well incorporated. Scoop heaping tablespoons of dough onto a cookie sheet and press flat with your fingers. Bake for 12–15 minutes or until edges are browned. Makes 10–14 cookies, depending on size.

Chocolate Chip Coconut Cookies

When I am in need of a good sugar fix, I make a batch of these. They are simple and taste heavenly. Even omnivores agree!
—Adina, Trinidad, Colorado

- egg replacer to equal 1 egg (pg 177)
- ½ cup vegan margarine
- ¾ cup sugar
- 1 tsp vanilla extract
- 1¼ cup flour
- ½ tsp baking powder
- ½ tsp baking soda
- ¼ tsp salt
- ½ cup shredded unsweetened coconut
- ¾ cup vegan chocolate chips

Preheat oven to 350°F (175°C). In a food processor, blend the egg replacer, margarine, sugar, and vanilla until smooth and set aside. In a large bowl, stir together the flour, baking powder and soda, salt, coconut, and chocolate chips. Add the margarine mixture and stir until well incorporated. Roll dough into balls, lay on cookie sheet, and bake for 10–12 minutes. Let cookies cool 5 minutes before removing from sheet. Makes 18–24 cookies.

Cinnamon Doughnut Holes

Ooooh, I bet if Tim Horton had tasted these, he would have given up hockey and opened a doughnut stand ... wait a second....

Coating:
- ¼ cup vegan margarine
- 1 tsp cinnamon
- ½ cup sugar

Doughnuts:
- 1⅓ cup flour
- 1 cup crispy rice-type cereal, coarsely crushed
- 2 tbsp sugar
- 1 tbsp baking powder
- ½ tsp salt
- ¼ cup vegetable shortening
- ½ cup vegan milk

Preheat oven to 425°F (220°C). In a small saucepan on medium-low heat, melt the margarine. Once liquefied, pour into a small bowl and set aside. In a small bowl, stir together the cinnamon and sugar and set aside. In a medium bowl, whisk together the flour, cereal, sugar, baking powder, and salt. Cut in shortening until mixture resembles coarse crumbs. Stir in "milk" until well blended and start rolling dough into 1-in (2½-cm) balls with your hands. Dip each ball in the melted margarine and then coat in the cinnamon-sugar. Place them in a lightly oiled 8x8-in (20x20-cm) baking pan so the balls are touching one another and bake for 16–18 minutes. Remove from oven and let cool before removing from pan. Makes 20–24 doughnut holes.

Wolffie's Pumpkin Pie

I'm thankful for pumpkins, for sugar, and for this pie. Don't worry that it won't look ready when you first take it out of the oven—it sets as it cools.

Topping:
- ¼ cup sugar
- ¼ cup flour
- ½ tsp cinnamon
- 2 tbsp vegan margarine
- ¼ cup walnuts or pecans, finely chopped

Filling:
- 1 14-oz (540-mL) can unsweetened pumpkin purée
- ½ cup vegan milk
- ¼ cup cornstarch
- ½ cup maple syrup
- ½ tsp salt
- ¼ cup sugar
- 1 tsp cinnamon
- 1 tsp ground ginger
- ¼ tsp allspice
- 1 tsp vanilla extract

- 1 9-in (23-cm) prepared pie crust (pg 172)

Preheat oven to 375°F (190°C). To prepare topping: In a small bowl, stir together the topping ingredients and set aside. To prepare filling: In a food processor, blend the filling ingredients until smooth. Pour filling into pie crust and sprinkle evenly with topping. Bake for 40–45 minutes. Remove from oven and let cool. Serve at room temperature. Makes 1 pie.

Fudge Pecan Pie

*Page 256 of **LDV** is getting awfully worn down. We love, love, love this recipe. —Paisley, Central Point, Oregon*

- ½ cup water
- ¼ cup vegan margarine
- 2 tbsp unsweetened cocoa powder
- ¾ cup vegan chocolate chips
- ⅓ cup flour
- 1 cup sugar
- ⅛ tsp of salt
- ½ cup vegan milk
- 1 tbsp vanilla extract
- 1 cup pecan halves
- 1 9-in (23-cm) prepared pie crust (pg 172)
- 2 tsp vegan milk

Preheat oven to 350°F (175°C). In a medium saucepan on high heat, bring water to a boil, then remove from heat. Whisk in the margarine, cocoa, and chocolate chips and continue to whisk until melted. Add flour, sugar, salt, ½ cup "milk," vanilla, and whisk until smooth. Stir in pecan halves and pour into pie crust. Bake for 55–60 minutes or until a toothpick or knife inserted in center comes out clean. Remove from oven and immediately brush the 2 tsp "milk" evenly over the top of pie. Let cool to room temperature before serving. Makes 1 pie.

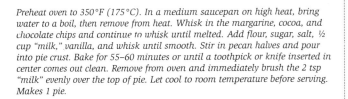

Pies

Baking

Chocolate Bourbon Pecan Pie

Formally referred to as "orgasm pie." One bite and you will understand. This pie is so elegant and rich, it has quite a reputation. Three words to describe it: "better—than—sex!"

- egg replacer to equal 2 eggs (pg 177)
- 2 tbsp molasses
- ½ cup corn syrup
- 2 tbsp bourbon
- 1 tsp vanilla extract
- ⅛ tsp salt
- 1½ cups pecans, chopped
- 1 cup vegan chocolate chips
- 4 whole pecans
- 1 9-in (23-cm) prepared pie crust (pg 172)

Preheat oven to 350°F (175°C). In a large bowl, mix together the egg replacer, molasses, syrup, bourbon, vanilla, and salt. Add the chopped pecans and chocolate chips and mix well. Pour into pie crust and arrange the whole pecans in the center of pie. Bake for 40–45 minutes. Makes 1 pie.

Chocolate Banana No-Bake Pie

No-bake pie! Sounds crazy, you say? Try it, we say.

- 1 cup vegan chocolate chips
- splash of vegan milk
- 1½ cups applesauce
- ½ cup sugar
- 4 bananas, chopped
- 1 9-in (23-cm) prepared pie crust (pg 172)

In a small double boiler, melt the chocolate chips with "milk," stirring chocolate until smooth. With a blender or food processor, blend the applesauce, sugar, bananas, and melted chocolate until well mixed. Pour into pie crust. Chill for at least 12 hours before eating. Makes 1 pie.

Nanaimo Bars

A Canadian dessert classic that originated in Nanaimo, British Columbia, in the 1950s. Included in the recipe is a little turmeric for an authentic Nanaimo Bar yellow center. Don't worry, you can't taste it, but boy-howdy is this recipe tasty! If you can't find ground flax seeds, you can substitute them and the water with half a mashed banana. And, if you can't find vegan graham cracker crumbs, try using firm tea biscuits that have been crumbled up.

Bottom layer:
- ½ cup vegan margarine
- ¼ cup sugar
- ⅓ cup cocoa powder
- 2 tbsp ground flax seeds
- 3 tbsp water
- ½ cup walnuts, finely chopped
- 1 cup unsweetened coconut, flaked
- 1¼ cup vegan graham cracker crumbs

Middle layer:
- ½ cup vegan margarine
- 2 tbsp vegan milk
- 1 tbsp corn starch
- 1 tsp vanilla extract
- ¼ tsp turmeric
- 2 cups powdered icing sugar

Top layer:
- 2 tbsp vegan margarine
- 4 1-oz (28-g) squares unsweetened chocolate

To prepare bottom layer: In a medium saucepan on low heat, melt the margarine and sugar, stirring to combine. Once liquefied, stir in the cocoa until smooth. Remove from heat. In a medium bowl, stir together the flax seeds, water, walnuts, coconut, and graham cracker crumbs. Add the chocolate sauce and stir well. Press mixture into an ungreased 8x8-in (20x20-cm) pan. Set aside.

To prepare top layer: In medium saucepan on low heat, melt the margarine. Add the chocolate and melt, stirring often to prevent burning. Remove from heat and set aside to pour over middle layer. You want sauce to be cooled but liquid to still spread easily.

To prepare middle layer and assemble bars: In a food processor or medium bowl, cream together the margarine, "milk," starch, vanilla, turmeric, and icing sugar until well mixed. Spread evenly over bottom layer. Spoon chocolate sauce evenly over middle layer and set pan in fridge immediately. Let chill for 2 + hours before cutting and serving. Makes 9 squares.

Chocolate Nut Energy Bars

The price of energy bars getting you down? This easy recipe can be made in a flash for only a few pennies.

- ½ cup dried fruit (e.g., raisins and cranberries)
- 1 cup walnuts
- ½ cup peanuts (or other nut)
- ½ cup cashews
- ½ cup pumpkin seeds
- ½ cup vegan chocolate chips
- 2 tbsp agave nectar or maple syrup
- ¼ tsp salt

In a food processor, blend all ingredients until mixture starts to pull away from the sides of the mixer and forms a dough. Transfer to a dry cutting board and shape into a loaf. Slice into bars. Wrap each bar in plastic wrap and keep in freezer until needed. Makes 6–10 bars.

Date Walnut Energy Bars

Gerry says these are *"mmmm, delicious!"*

- 2 cups dates
- ½ cup dried fruit (e.g., cranberries and blueberries)
- 1 cup walnuts
- ½ cup hemp seeds (or sesame seeds)
- ¼ tsp salt
- ½ cup rolled oat flakes

In a small bowl, pour hot water over dates and let sit 15–30 minutes, then drain. In a food processor, blend dates and remaining ingredients until mixture starts to pull away from the sides of the mixer and forms a dough. Transfer to a dry cutting board and shape into a loaf. Slice into bars. Wrap each bar in plastic wrap and keep in freezer until needed. Makes 6–10 bars.

Righteous Orbs

These orbs will help keep your energy up for those late night quests. If you can't find hemp seeds, then you can use finely shredded coconut or sesame seeds.

- ⅓ cup shelled hemp seeds
- 2 cups nuts of your choice (walnuts, almonds, pecans, etc.)
- 1 cup raisins
- 1 tsp cinnamon
- ¼ tsp salt
- 1 tbsp oil (e.g., flax or hemp)
- 2 tbsp agave nectar or maple syrup

Place a sheet of parchment or wax paper on a large plate or cookie sheet. Set aside. Measure out seeds onto a small plate and set aside. In a food processor, blend the remaining ingredients until mixture starts to pull away from the sides of the mixer and forms a dough. Transfer dough to a large bowl and scoop out spoonfuls to form 16 golf ball-sized balls. Roll each ball in hemp seeds until coated. Place on lined plate or cookie sheet and refrigerate for 1 hour before serving. Makes 16 orbs.

Bars

Baking

Chocolate Chip Bars

I love these bars so much, Sarah. I bring them to work with me and everyone in the office eats them up and can't believe they're vegan.
—Mary, Yorkton, Saskatchewan

- 3½ cups flour
- 1½ tsp baking powder
- ½ tsp baking soda
- ½ tsp salt
- 1½ cups sugar
- 1 cup oil
- 1 tsp vanilla extract
- 1 cup vegan milk
- 1 cup vegan chocolate chips or carob chips

Preheat oven to 350°F (175°C). In a large bowl, stir together the flour, baking powder and soda, salt, and sugar. Add the oil, vanilla, "milk," and chocolate or carob chips and mix gently until just mixed. Pour mixture into a 9x13-in (23x33-cm) pan and bake for 25–30 minutes until a toothpick or knife inserted in center comes out clean. Let cool for 10 minutes before cutting into bars. Makes 12 bars.

Microwave Banana Oatmeal Chocolate Chip Bars

The good news is that you can make this recipe in a few minutes. The aroma alone will have you drooling ... but the bad news is that you have to wait for the bars to cool before you can eat one.

- ½ banana
- ½ cup sugar
- ¼ cup vegan margarine
- 1 tsp vanilla extract
- ¼ cup vegan milk
- ½ cup flour
- ½ cup rolled oat flakes
- 1 tsp baking powder
- ¼ tsp salt
- ⅓ cup vegan chocolate chips

In a large bowl, mash the banana into the sugar, margarine, vanilla, and "milk" and mix well. Add the flour, oats, baking powder, and salt and mix well. Spread evenly in a lightly oiled, microwave-safe loaf pan. Sprinkle with chocolate chips. Cook in the microwave on high for 4–5 minutes. Let cool before cutting and serving. Makes 8 bars.

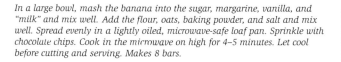

Bars

Baking

Cracker Jane's Popcorn

Don't get in trouble with your dentist. Be sure to floss your teeth after you eat this creation.

- 8 cups popped popcorn
- 2 cups peanuts (or 1 cup peanuts and 1 cup other nuts)
- ½ cup vegan margarine
- 1 cup sugar
- ½ cup dark corn syrup
- ½ tsp salt
- ½ tsp baking powder

Preheat oven to 250°F (120°C). In a large bowl, combine the popcorn and nuts. Set aside. In a medium saucepan on high heat, bring the margarine, sugar, syrup, and salt to a boil. Reduce heat to simmer for 5 minutes, stirring occasionally. Whisk in baking powder until smooth. Pour over popcorn and stir until well mixed. Pour into a lightly oiled 9x13-in (23x33-cm) pan. Bake for one hour, stirring occasionally. Cool and break up into small chunks. Makes approx. 6 cups.

Auntie Bonnie's Wacky Cake

This cake never fails and I have had people say it's the best chocolate cake they've ever eaten. Cake is one of the things people think vegans don't do well. This recipe proves them wrong.
—**Fiona, Accrington, England**

- 1½ cups flour
- 4 tbsp cocoa or carob powder
- 1 tsp baking powder
- 1 tsp baking soda
- ½ tsp salt
- 1 cup sugar
- 1½ tsp vanilla extract
- 1 tbsp vinegar
- ⅓ cup oil
- 1 cup cold water

Preheat oven to 325°F (165°C). In a large bowl, stir together the flour, cocoa, baking powder and soda, and salt. Add the remaining ingredients and mix gently until just mixed. Pour into a lightly oiled 8-in (20-cm) cake pan and bake for 40–45 minutes until a toothpick or fork inserted in center comes out clean. When cooled, frost with icing of your choice and serve. Makes 1 cake.

Cakes

Baking

Chocolate Upside-Down Pudding Cake

This is so easy and so absolutely scrumptious. This is one of the easiest desserts to make and will impress any vegan naysayers!
—Sheila, Lake Country, British Columbia

Cake:
- 1 cup flour
- 1 tbsp baking powder
- ¼ cup cocoa powder
- ¼ tsp salt
- ½ cup sugar
- ½ cup vegan margarine
- ½ cup vegan milk
- 1 tsp vanilla extract

Sauce:
- ¾ cup sugar
- ¼ cup cocoa powder
- 2 cups boiling water

Preheat oven to 350°F (175°C).

To prepare cake: In a large bowl, stir together the flour, baking powder, cocoa, and salt. Add the sugar, margarine, "milk," and vanilla, and mix gently until just mixed. Spread in a lightly oiled casserole dish or 9-in (23-cm) loaf pan. Set aside.

To prepare sauce and assemble cake: In a medium bowl, mix together the sugar and cocoa. Sprinkle evenly on top of the cake. Carefully pour the boiling water over top. DO NOT MIX THIS! It will do its own thing in the oven. Bake for 40 minutes. To serve, scoop out portions and serve in a bowl with vegan ice cream. Makes 1 pudding cake.

Rene's Tomato Soup Spice Cake

This is my favorite recipe to make for cooking demos and veg festivals. The ingredients can be found anywhere … and the shock value of opening a can of tomato soup to make this cake is worth the price of admission. Love, love, love this recipe. Thanks, Rene! (Check out the icing for this cake on pg 174.)

- 1 10-oz (285-mL) can condensed tomato soup
- 2 tbsp oil
- 1 cup sugar
- 1 tsp baking soda
- 1 tsp baking powder
- 1 tsp cinnamon
- ½ tsp ground cloves
- 1½ cups flour
- ½ cup raisins (optional)

Preheat oven to 350°F (175°C). Lightly oil and flour a Bundt or 8-in (20-cm) round cake pan and set aside. In a large bowl, stir together the tomato soup, oil, and sugar. Add the baking soda and powder, cinnamon, cloves, and flour and mix well. Stir in raisins and pour batter into pan. Bake for 25–30 minutes or until a toothpick or knife inserted in center comes out clean. Let cool for 10–15 minutes before removing from pan. Makes 1 cake.

Cakes

Baking

Yella Cake

I messed with your Yella Cake recipe from **LDV** *to make it a marble cake. Once the batter is done, I reserve about ¾ and put it into a medium bowl and add 1½ tbsp cocoa powder and stir until mixed. I scoop spoonfuls of the chocolate batter evenly into the yellow batter in the pan and draw a knife a few times through the length of the batter. Don't over do it or it will mix too much. Four to five lines is good. Yum!*
—Holly, Ottawa, Ontario

- ¾ cup sugar
- ¼ cup vegan margarine
- egg replacer to equal 1 egg (pg 177)
- 1 tsp vanilla extract
- 1½ cups flour
- 1¼ tsp baking powder
- ¼ tsp salt
- ¾ cup vegan milk

Preheat oven to 350°F (175°C). Lightly oil a 9-in (23-cm) round cake pan and set aside. In a large bowl, cream together the sugar, margarine, egg replacer, and vanilla. Add the flour, baking powder, salt, and "milk," and stir gently until just mixed. Spread evenly into pan and bake for 30–35 minutes, until a toothpick or knife inserted in center comes out clean. Let cool for 10–15 minutes before removing from pan. Cool completely before frosting with icing of your choice. Makes 1 cake.

Apricot Cheesecake

This is a "day before" recipe, meaning you have to make it the day before you want to serve it. You will also need a springform pan. If you can't find vegan graham cracker crumbs, then use firm tea biscuits and grind them up in a food processor. This recipe is so amazing that even my stepmum (who does *not* like tofu) requested it for her birthday.

Crust:
- 1½ cups vegan graham cracker crumbs
- ¼ cup vegan margarine, melted
- ¼ cup sugar

Glaze:
- 1 cup apricot fruit spread (or preserves)
- 1 tbsp corn starch
- ¼ cup water

Filling:
- 2 12-oz (300-g) pkgs soft or silken tofu
- 2 cups vegan cream cheese
- ¾ cup sugar
- 1 tbsp vanilla extract
- 1 tbsp lemon juice
- 1 tsp lemon rind, finely grated
- ½ tsp salt
- ¼ cup flour

Preheat oven to 300°F (150°C).

To prepare crust: Lightly oil a 9-in (23-cm) springform pan and set aside. In a small mixing bowl, stir together graham cracker crumbs, melted margarine, and sugar. Press mixture firmly into the bottom of prepared pan and set aside.

To prepare filling: In a food processor, process the tofu, "cream cheese," sugar, vanilla, lemon juice and rind, salt, and flour until smooth. Pour evenly over crust and bake for 75 minutes. Remove from oven and place on cooling rack; allow to cool completely in pan. Cover and refrigerate overnight.

To prepare glaze and assemble cake: In a small saucepan, bring the fruit spread, starch, and water to a boil. Reduce heat and simmer for 4–6 minutes, whisking constantly. Remove from heat and cool completely. Remove the sides of the pan from the cake and spread glaze evenly over top. Refrigerate for at least 1 hour before serving. Makes 1 cake.

Cakes

Baking

Country Carrot Cake

My all-time favorite cake. I had it for my eighteenth birthday, topped with the delicious Cream Cheese Icing (pg 173). Even my non-vegan, carrot cake aficionado brother approves. —Alicia, Florence, Kentucky

- 1½ cups flour
- ¾ cup sugar
- 2 tsp baking powder
- 1 tsp cinnamon
- ¼ tsp salt
- ¾ cup vegan milk
- 2 tsp vanilla extract
- ¼ cup oil
- egg replacer to equal 1 egg (pg 177)
- ½ cup carrot, finely grated
- 1 tsp fresh ginger, grated

Preheat oven to 350°F (175°C). In a large bowl, stir together the flour, sugar, baking powder, cinnamon, and salt. Add remaining ingredients and mix gently until just mixed. Pour into a lightly oiled 9-in (23-cm) cake pan and bake for 25–30 minutes, until a toothpick or knife inserted in center comes out clean. Makes 1 cake.

Blueberry Dilip

Not quite a crisp, not quite a crumble—this recipe from Dilip in Chapel Hill, North Carolina is simply that ... a Dilip. A yummy, blueberry Dilip!

- ¼ cup vegan margarine
- 1 cup flour
- ½ cup sugar
- 2 tsp baking powder
- ½ tsp cinnamon
- ¼ tsp salt
- ⅛ tsp nutmeg
- ¾ cup vegan milk
- ¼ cup sugar
- 1 tsp ground ginger
- 4 cups blueberries

Preheat oven to 350°F (175°C). Put the margarine into an 8-in (20-cm) baking dish and place in oven while it's preheating. In a medium bowl, stir together the flour, sugar, baking powder, cinnamon, salt, and nutmeg. Add the "milk," stir well, and set aside. Once the margarine has melted, pour the flour mixture into the baking dish without mixing it into the margarine. In a medium bowl, stir together the remaining ¼ cup sugar, ginger, and blueberries and pour over batter (do not stir). Bake for 50–55 minutes. Serve warm. Makes 2 large or 4 small servings.

Fruit

Baking

Fruit Dipping Sauce

This recipe will knock the attitude right out of any tofu naysayers. A perfect dipping sauce for fresh fruit or even tossed into a fruit salad. Don't tell them it's tofu until after they've tried it … then help them lift their jaws off the floor.

- 1 12-oz (300-g) pkg soft or silken tofu
- ¼ cup maple syrup
- ¾ tsp cinnamon

In a food processor, combine all ingredients and blend until smooth. Makes approx. 1½ cups.

Microwave Apple Crisp

Are you dying for a piece of Grandma's apple pie? But you're stuck somewhere without an oven? Here's a solution!

- 2 apples of your choice, cored and chopped
- 3 tbsp vegan margarine
- ¼ cup sugar
- 4 tbsp flour
- 1 tsp cinnamon
- ½ tsp nutmeg
- ½ cup rolled oat flakes

Arrange apple pieces in an 8x8-in (20x20-cm) microwave-safe dish. In a bowl, combine the remaining ingredients. Sprinkle mixture evenly over apples. Cook in the microwave on high for 10–12 minutes. Let stand 2 minutes before serving. Makes 2 large or 4 small servings.

Baking

Fruit

Beautiful Blueberry Strudel

Phyllo (also spelled filo or fillo) pastry is tissue-paper-thin layers of pastry dough. Found in the freezer section of your grocery store.

- ¼ cup vegan margarine, melted
- 2 cups blueberries
- ¼ cup sugar
- 2 tbsp corn starch
- 3 sheets phyllo pastry, thawed
- 3 tbsp bread crumbs
- 1 tbsp sugar

Preheat oven to 375°F (190°C). Lightly oil a cookie sheet and set aside. In a small saucepan, melt the margarine. While margarine is melting, in a small bowl, stir together the blueberries, sugar, and starch until well combined. Set aside. Lay a clean dishtowel down on counter. Unroll phyllo pastry, remove one sheet, and lay on top of dishtowel. Brush evenly with 1 tbsp of melted margarine then evenly spread 1 tbsp of the breadcrumbs over top. Layer another sheet on top and repeat process until done. Spoon blueberry filling along the long edge of the phyllo, making a large border around the edge. Carefully turn long edge of phyllo up to cover fruit filling and then fold in the sides. Carefully roll up the pastry and place on cookie sheet folded side down. Brush top lightly with remaining margarine, sprinkle with 1 tbsp of sugar, and bake for 35–40 minutes. Let cool for 4–6 minutes before serving. Makes 2 large or 4 small servings.

Basic Flaky Pie Crust

This is the easiest and most basic pie crust ever invented. If you're making a pie that has a top, make sure you double this recipe.

- 1¼ cups flour
- ¼ tsp salt
- ½ cup vegetable shortening
- 3 tbsp very cold water

In a large bowl, stir together the flour and salt. Cut the shortening into the flour mixture until well mixed, then add the water. Mix together until a dough forms. On a lightly floured surface, knead for a minute or two and then roll into a ball. Wrap dough in wax paper and chill for 30 minutes. Roll the dough into a pie crust. Makes 1 crust.

"Anything Goes" Icing

A versatile classic.

- ¼ cup vegan margarine
- 2¼ cups powdered icing sugar
- 2 tbsp vegan milk
- 1 tsp "anything goes" extract (lemon, peppermint, etc.)

In a food processor or medium bowl, mix together all ingredients until smooth. Makes approx. 1½ cups.

Cream Cheese Icing

You can find vegan cream cheese at most health food stores and, man, is it awesome!

- 1 cup vegan cream cheese
- 2 tbsp vegan margarine
- 1 cup powdered icing sugar

In a food processor or medium bowl, mix all ingredients until smooth. Makes approx. 1¼ cups.

Basic Cake Glaze

This glaze can be used on cakes, cupcakes, and more. Try rolling the Cinnamon Doughnut Holes (pg 151) in it. The flavor is up to you: mint, lemon, orange, maple extract—get crazy!

- ¼ cup vegan margarine, melted
- 2 cups powdered icing sugar
- 2 tbsp vegan milk
- extract/flavoring of your choice (to taste)

In a medium bowl, stir together all ingredients until smooth and creamy. Add a little more "milk" if you want a thinner glaze. Drizzle over a cooled cake and refrigerate for at least 1 hour before serving. Makes approx. 1½ cups.

Miscellaneous

Baking

173

Chocolate Glaze

This easy chocolate glaze can be poured over a cake or a freshly baked pan of brownies. Just remember to cool your baking completely before you glaze. Once poured, you can garnish with minced nuts or fancy cake sprinkles.

- 1 cup vegan chocolate chips
- ⅔ cup vegan margarine

In a small double boiler on medium heat, melt the chocolate chips and margarine, stirring until smooth and creamy. Let cool a little before spooning over cake or brownies. Refrigerate to set glaze for at least 1 hour before serving. Makes approx. 1¼ cups.

Rene's Vanilla Frosting

Rene uses this fabu icing on his Tomato Soup Spice Cake (pg 165).

- ½ cup vegan margarine
- 2 cups powdered icing sugar
- 2 tbsp vegan milk
- 1 tbsp vanilla extract
- ⅛ tsp salt

In a food processor or medium bowl, mix together all ingredients until smooth. Makes approx. 3 cups.

Banana-Rama Whipped Cream

Enjoy this rich, creamy sauce over fruit salad, oatmeal, even pancakes!

- 1 large banana
- 2 tbsp oil
- 1 tsp vanilla extract
- ½ tsp lemon juice

In a blender or food processor, blend all ingredients until smooth and creamy. Use immediately. Makes approx. ½ cup.

Soymilk Whipped Cream

You must use soymilk in this whip-tastic recipe. Whip it! Whip it good!

- ¼ cup soymilk
- 2–4 tbsp sweetener
- ½ tsp vanilla extract
- 1 tsp cornstarch
- ½ cup oil

In a blender or food processor, blend together the "milk," sweetener, vanilla, and cornstarch. Slowly drizzle in the oil while the blender is running. Blend until smooth and creamy. Chill for 1 hour before using. Makes approx. ¾ cup.

Egg Replacers

Which came first? The vegan or the egg? Replacing eggs in vegan baking is as easy as 1, 2 ... wait ... I have five alternatives for you.

Flax Seed Egg Replacer ⸺▶	2 tbsp ground flax seeds + 3 tbsp water
Tofu Egg Replacer ⸺▶	¼ cup blended soft tofu
Ener-G Egg Replacer ⸺▶	1½ tsp Ener-G Egg Replacer Powder + 2 tbsp water
Banana Egg Replacer ⸺▶	½ banana, mashed well
Applesauce Egg Replacer ⸺▶	3 tbsp applesauce

Milk Alternatives

Are you stuck in the middle of nowhere with no hope in heck of finding a carton of soy or rice milk? These six quick and easy recipes can help you when you're in a pinch. Keep in mind that each "milk" recipe below has a distinct flavor, so if you're making cookies, try the nut butter milk. Or if you want to use it over cereal, try the banana milk. You dig where I'm coming from?

Quick Nut Butter Milk

- 2 tbsp nut butter (e.g., peanut or almond)
- 1 cup water
- 1 tsp–1 tbsp sugar (optional)

In a blender (or container with tight-fitting lid), mix (or shake) ingredients until smooth. Use within 24 hours. Makes approx. 1¼ cups.

Quick Sesame Milk

- 2 tbsp tahini
- 1 cup water
- 1 tsp–1 tbsp sugar (optional)

In a blender (or container with tight-fitting lid), mix (or shake) ingredients until smooth. Use within 24 hours. Makes approx. 1¼ cups.

Quick Banana Milk

- 1 banana
- 1 cup water
- 1 tsp–1 tbsp sugar (optional)

In a blender, mix ingredients until smooth. Use within 24 hours. Makes approx. 1 cup.

Quick Oat Milk

- 3 tbsp cooked oatmeal
- 1 cup water
- 1 tsp–1 tbsp sugar (optional)

In a blender, mix ingredients until smooth. Makes approx. 1¼ cups.

Faux

Quick Rice Milk

- ¼ cup cooked rice
- 1 cup water
- 1 tsp–1 tbsp sugar (optional)

In a blender, mix ingredients until smooth.
Use within 24 hours. Makes approx. 1¼ cups.

Quick Hemp Milk

- ¼ cup shelled hemp seeds
- 1 cup water
- 1 tsp–1 tbsp sugar (optional)

In a blender, mix until smooth.
Use within 24 hours. Makes approx. 1¼ cups.

Faux

Faux Feta Cheese

I love this recipe in Greek salad or on pizza.

- 1 cup firm tofu, cubed or crumbled
- 2 tbsp oil (e.g., flax or hemp)
- 2 tbsp water
- ¼ cup red wine vinegar
- 1 tsp salt
- 1½ tbsp dried basil
- ¼ tsp dried oregano
- ¼ tsp dried dill
- ¼ tsp black pepper

In a medium bowl, mix together all the ingredients. Marinate tofu for at least 1 hour before using. Makes approx. ¾ cup.

Faux Sour Cream

And you thought you'd never have sour cream again....

- 1 12-oz (300-g) pkg soft or silken tofu
- 1 tbsp oil
- 1 tbsp lemon juice
- 2 tsp apple cider vinegar
- 1 tsp sugar
- ½ tsp salt
- 1 tbsp Braggs or tamari

With a blender or food processor, blend all ingredients until smooth and creamy. Makes approx. 1 cup.

Tofu Mayonnaise

Fear not—it's time to welcome mayonnaise back into your life.

- ¾ cup soft or medium tofu
- 2 tbsp lemon juice or apple cider vinegar
- ½ tsp salt
- ⅛ tsp black pepper
- 2 tbsp oil

With a blender or food processor, blend (on high) all ingredients until thick and creamy. Makes approx. 1½ cups.

Soymilk Mayonnaise

You must use soymilk in this recipe!

- ¾ cup soymilk
- 1½ tbsp lemon juice or apple cider vinegar
- ¾ tsp salt
- ⅛ tsp black pepper
- ¾ cup oil

With a blender or food processor, blend (on high) the "milk," lemon juice, salt, and pepper for 1 minute. Add the oil gradually while blending until mayonnaise thickens. Makes approx. 1½ cups.

Faux Cheese

Sarah! I know there are a ton of faux cheese recipes out there, but this one is mine. Agar can be found in most Asian markets. I hope you like it!
—**Cheryl, Salt Lake City, Utah**

- ¾ cup cashews
- ¼ small orange bell pepper, roughly chopped
- 1 tsp salt
- 1 tsp onion powder
- ½ tsp oil
- 2 tbsp lemon juice
- 1 cup water
- 4 tsp powdered agar (or ¼ cup flakes)

In a food processor, blend the cashews, bell pepper, salt, onion powder, oil, and lemon juice until smooth. In a small saucepan on high heat, bring the water to a boil. Reduce heat and whisk in agar, stirring often until it starts to thicken. Spoon into food processor and blend with cashew mixture until smooth. Spread evenly in square or rectangular container and refrigerate for at least 1 hour before using. Makes approx. 16 oz (455 g).

Faux Parmesan Cheese

Simply the world's greatest faux cheese topping. Enjoy.

- ¼ cup nutritional yeast flakes
- ¼ cup sesame seeds, toasted
- ¼ tsp salt

With a blender, food processor, or coffee grinder, grind all ingredients until completely milled. Makes approx. ½ cup.

Faux

Faux Chicken

Try making Jay-Lo's Fried Chicken (pg 117) with this recipe.

• Basic Instant Gluten or Basic Gluten from Scratch (pg 186-187)

Broth:
• 2 cups water
• ¼ cup nutritional yeast
• 2 tbsp Braggs or tamari
• 1 tsp onion powder
• 1 tsp dried sage
• ½ tsp dried thyme
• ½ tsp salt
• ¼ tsp celery seeds

In a large saucepan on high heat, bring all broth ingredients to a boil. Slice gluten into steaks, chunks, or strips and drop carefully into broth. Reduce heat, cover with lid, and simmer for 50–60 minutes, stirring every 10 minutes, until broth has reduced completely. Use "chicken" immediately in your recipe of choice or store in the refrigerator (for up to 6 days) or the freezer (for up to 6 months). For a chewier texture, once you've boiled the "chicken," bake it at 350°F (175°C) in a lightly oiled baking sheet for 30 minutes. Makes 2 large or 4 small servings.

Faux Beef

Cut gluten into thin strips and throw it in a stir-fry! Yum.

- Basic Instant Gluten or Basic Gluten from Scratch (pg 186–187)

Broth:
- 2 cups water
- ¼ cup Braggs or tamari
- 2 tsp vegan Worcestershire sauce
- 2 tbsp nutritional yeast
- 1 tsp onion powder
- ½ tsp cayenne pepper
- ¼ tsp dried sage

In a large saucepan, bring all broth ingredients to a boil. Slice gluten into steaks, chunks, or strips and drop carefully into broth. Reduce heat, cover with lid, and let simmer for 50–60 minutes, stirring every 10 minutes, until broth has reduced completely. Use "beef" immediately in your recipe of choice or store in the refrigerator (for up to 6 days) or the freezer (for up to 6 months). For a chewier texture, once you've boiled the "beef," bake it at 350°F (175°C) in a lightly oiled baking dish for 30 minutes. Makes 2 large or 4 small servings.

Faux

Tofu Jerky

I love Tofu Jerky! This recipe is perfect for road trips. I will sometimes double or triple this recipe. —Amy, cyberspace

- 1 lb (455 g) extra firm tofu, drained
- ½ cup Braggs or tamari
- 3–4 tbsp liquid smoke
- ⅛ cup water
- 1 tbsp onion powder
- 1 tsp garlic powder, or 1 garlic clove, minced
- ½–1 tbsp black pepper
- 1 tsp sugar

Cut the tofu into long narrow strips about ¼ in (½ cm) thick. They may look big, but they will shrink during baking. In a small bowl, whisk together the remaining ingredients. Place tofu strips in a shallow baking pan or on a cookie sheet and pour the marinade over them. Marinate in refrigerator for several hours, or overnight for best results. Cook the tofu in a food dehydrator (follow manual's directions) or bake in the oven for about 4–6 hours at 200°F (95°C). Turn the tofu over once every hour so it bakes evenly. Continue until the texture is very chewy, but not crispy. Makes 8–12 strips.

Basic Instant Gluten

Cook this dough in either of the mock-meat flavors (pg 183-184) or in a broth of your own invention. In *LDV*, there are also recipes for sausage, turkey, fish, and ham flavors.

- ½ cup instant vital wheat gluten flour
- ½ cup water

In a medium bowl, stir together the ingredients until dough becomes elastic. Knead for 5 minutes and set aside. Choose a mock meat flavoring (pg 183-184) to add to dough. Makes 2 large or 4 small servings.

Gluten from Scratch

This recipe might seem complicated, but if you can't find or don't have gluten flour, what are you going to do? You work with what you have, so lets get our hands gooey! Let's go!

- 2 cups whole wheat flour
- 2 cups all-purpose flour
- 1¾ cups water

In a large bowl, stir together the flours. Add the water and mix, then knead until well combined. Cover bowl with cloth and let sit for 30 minutes. Wet hands and knead dough for 1 minute, then return to bowl. Place bowl in sink and add cold water until bowl is filled. Squeeze dough with your hands until water turns cloudy (don't worry if it falls apart ... just keep kneading). Carefully pour off water (holding back dough with your hands) and fill bowl again with cold water. Repeat process of squeezing dough in fresh cold water 4–6 times until dough starts to solidify and water is no longer cloudy. Repeat process 2 more times, alternating between warm and cold water. Start stretching and pulling the dough as you rinse it. Once it becomes a cohesive, elastic mass (similar to bubble gum), rinse one final time in cold water. Squeeze any remaining water from the dough and set aside. Choose a faux meat flavoring (pg 183-184) to use with your dough. Makes 2 large or 4 small servings.

Odds & Sods

KEEP AN EYE OUT

Gomashio

Gomashio can be used to season soups, salads, pasta…. I sometimes eat it with a spoon!

- 1 cup raw sesame seeds
- 1 tsp sea salt
- 1 tsp kelp powder
- ½ sheet nori (dried seaweed), cut or torn into small pieces

In a dry frying pan over medium-high heat, stir or shake the sesame seeds continually for 3–5 minutes, until seeds start to pop and brown. Remove from heat and let cool completely. In a food processor, combine cooled seeds with remaining ingredients and grind for 5–10 seconds (you don't want the seeds to become powder, just lightly ground). Store in an airtight container. Makes approx. 1 cup.

Kitchen Cupboard Garam Masala

Just raid your pantry. I'm sure you'll have most of these spices on hand.

- 2 tbsp cumin
- 2 tbsp ground coriander seeds
- 2 tsp black pepper
- 1 tsp ground cardamom
- 1 tsp ground ginger
- ¼ tsp allspice

In a small jar, combine all ingredients. Cap and shake well before using. Makes approx. ⅓ cup.

All-Purpose Spice

This spice mixture adds a quick and powerful punch to whatever you add it to.

- 2 tbsp chili powder
- 2 tsp onion powder
- 2 tsp cumin
- 2 tsp garlic powder
- 2 tsp oregano
- 1 tsp paprika
- 1 tsp salt
- ½ tsp cayenne pepper

In a small jar, combine all the ingredients. Cap and shake well before using. Makes approx. ¼ cup.

No-Salt Shaker

Looking for an alternative to the great white powder? No need for rehab. Just try this no-salt seasoning. Come on. Try it. Everyone else is.

- 3 tsp garlic powder
- 2 tsp onion powder
- 2 tsp dried thyme
- 2 tsp paprika
- 2 tsp black pepper
- 2 tsp dry mustard
- 1 tsp celery seeds

In a small jar, combine all ingredients. Cap and shake well before using. Makes approx. ¼ cup.

Cure-All Ginger Tea

Not feeling well? This always does the trick for me.

- 3 cups water
- 3 tbsp fresh ginger, grated
- ⅛ tsp cayenne pepper
- sweetener (to taste)

In a medium saucepan on high heat, bring the water to a boil. Add the ginger and cayenne and reduce heat to simmer for 20 minutes and strain. Add the sweetener. Drink and be healthy. Makes 2 servings.

Savory Miso Drink

A wonderful broth for when you're feeling under the weather; or over the weather for that matter.

- 1 tbsp miso (light or dark)
- 1 mug boiling water

Mix ingredients in mug until miso dissolves. Drink up! Makes 1 serving.

In a Pinch

20% OFF
ALL Stuff!

SHOP
'TIL YOU
DROP

Did you forget your toothpaste? These three homemade toothpaste recipes can be made when you're in a pinch.

Plain Toothpaste

- 1 tsp baking soda
- ¼ tsp salt

In a cup or small bowl, mix together the ingredients.
Dip damp toothbrush into the mixture and brush teeth.

Cinnamon Toothpaste

- 1 tsp baking soda
- ¼ tsp salt
- ⅛ tsp cinnamon
- 1 drop tea tree oil (optional)

In a cup or small bowl, mix together the ingredients.
Dip damp toothbrush into the mixture and brush teeth.

Peppermint-Clove Toothpaste

- 1 tsp baking soda
- ¼ tsp sea salt
- 1 drop clove essential oil
- 1 drop peppermint essential oil

In a cup or small bowl, mix together the ingredients.
Dip damp toothbrush into mixture and brush teeth.

Makeup Remover

Did you forget your makeup remover?

Apply vegetable oil, vegetable shortening, or vitamin-E oil
to skin and tissue off.

Measurement Equivalents

**Without this ...
I'd go crazy!**

Measurement Conversions

Teaspoon	Tablespoon	Cup	Fluid Ounce
3 tsp	1 tbsp	¹⁄₁₆ cup	½ oz
6 tsp	2 tbsp	⅛ cup	1 oz
12 tsp	4 tbsp	¼ cup	2 oz
16 tsp	5⅓ tbsp	⅓ cup	2⅔ oz
24 tsp	8 tbsp	½ cup	4 oz
32 tsp	10⅔ tbsp	⅔ cup	5⅓ oz
36 tsp	12 tbsp	¾ cup	6 oz
48 tsp	16 tbsp	1 cup	8 oz

*If you don't have measuring spoons,
you can always use your hands:*

Pound	Ounce
¼ lb	4 oz
½ lb	8 oz
¾ lb	12 oz
1 lb	16 oz

Hand Measurement	Tsp/Tbsp/Cup
1 pinch	⅛ tsp
3 pinches	½ tsp
5 pinches	1 tsp
palm of hand	1 tbsp
1 cupped hand	1 cup

PLACES TO SEE
THINGS TO DO

198

PLACES TO SEE
THINGS TO DO

RESTAURANTS
To Visit

SECRETSOCIETYOFVEGANS.CO.UK
GOVEGAN.NET

BOOKS TO READ

ADDRESSES

NAME 👉 _____
ADDRESS: _____
_____ ☎ ....
BIRTHDAY: _____
EMAIL: ....

NAME 👉 _____
ADDRESS: _____
_____ ☎ ....
BIRTHDAY: _____
EMAIL: ....

204

NAME 👉 _____

ADDRESS: _____

☎ ....

BIRTHDAY: _____

EMAIL: ....

NAME 👉 _____

ADDRESS: _____

☎ ....

BIRTHDAY: _____

EMAIL: ....

NAME ☞ _____

ADDRESS: _____

_____ ☎ ....

_____ BIRTHDAY: _____

EMAIL: ....

NAME ☞ _____

ADDRESS: _____

_____ ☎ ....

_____ BIRTHDAY: _____

EMAIL: ....

NAME 👉 _____
ADDRESS: _____
_____
☎ ....
_____ BIRTHDAY: _____
EMAIL: ....

NAME 👉 _____
ADDRESS: _____
_____
☎ ....
_____ BIRTHDAY: _____
EMAIL: ....

NAME 👉 _____

ADDRESS: _____

☎ ....

BIRTHDAY: _____

EMAIL: ....

NAME 👉 _____

ADDRESS: _____

☎ ....

BIRTHDAY: _____

EMAIL: ....

NAME 👉 _____

ADDRESS: _____

_____

📞 ....

_____ BIRTHDAY: _____

EMAIL: ....

NAME 👉 _____

ADDRESS: _____

_____

📞 ....

_____ BIRTHDAY: _____

EMAIL: ....

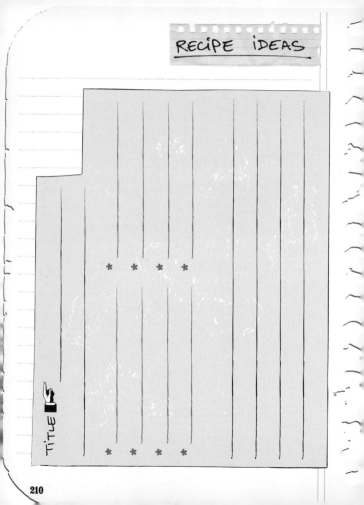

TITLE

* * * *

* * * *

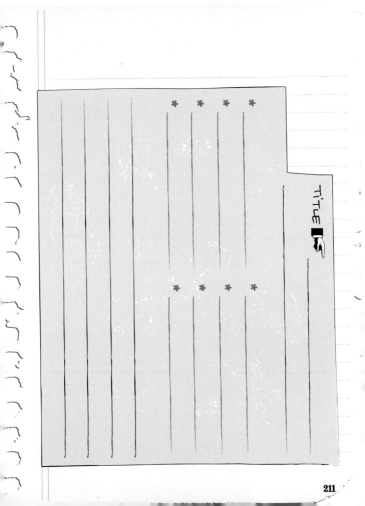

TITLE

*   *   *   *

*   *   *   *

TITLE

*   *   *   *

*   *   *   *

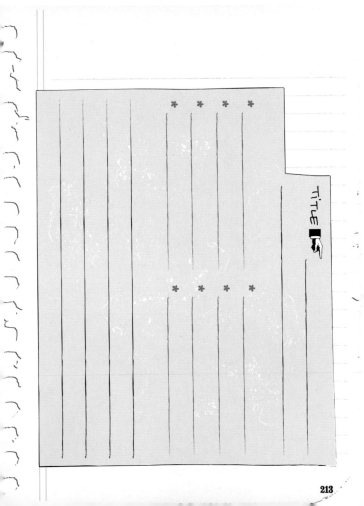

TITLE

213

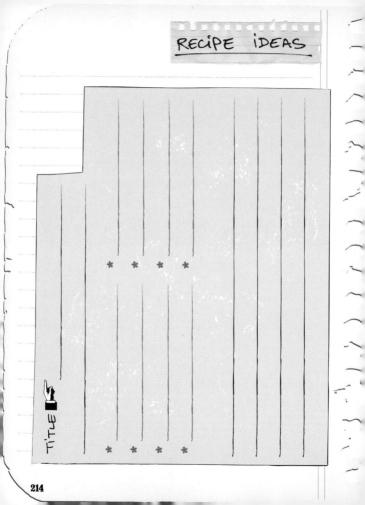

TITLE

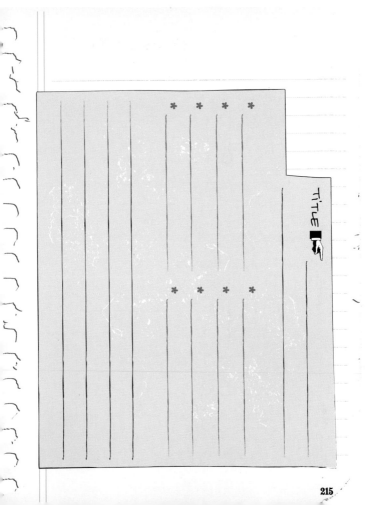

TITLE

* * * *

* * * *

215

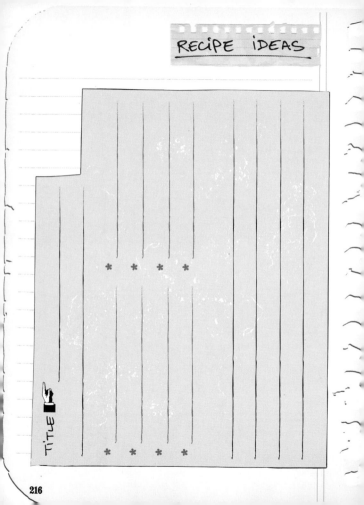

TITLE

* * * *

* * * *

NOTES

Recipes & Main Ingredients